GLASGOW ACADEMY ROLL OF HONOUR
1914-1918

PUBLISHED BY

JACKSON, WYLIE & CO., GLASGOW
Publishers to the University
—

LONDON : SIMPKIN, MARSHALL LTD.
Cambridge - - Bowes and Bowes
Oxford - - - Basil Blackwell, Ltd.
Edinburgh - - Douglas and Foulis
New York - - The Macmillan Co.
Toronto - - - The Macmillan Co. of Canada
Sydney - - - Angus and Robertson
—

MCMXXXIII

THE SCHOOL

GLASGOW ACADEMY

ROLL OF HONOUR

*Former Members of the School who
served in the Great War*

1914–1918

GLASGOW
JACKSON, WYLIE & CO.
PUBLISHERS TO THE UNIVERSITY
1933

TO · THE · MEMORY · OF
THOSE · FORMER · MEMBERS · OF · THIS · SCHOOL · WHO · LEFT
ALL · THAT · WAS · DEAR · TO · THEM · ENDURED · HARDSHIP
FACED · DANGER · AND · FINALLY · PASSED · OUT · OF · THE
SIGHT · OF · MAN · BY · THE · PATH · OF · DUTY · AND · SELF
SACRIFICE · GIVING · UP · THEIR · OWN · LIVES · THAT
OTHERS · MIGHT · LIVE · IN · FREEDOM. · LET · THOSE · WHO
COME · AFTER · SEE · TO · IT · THAT · THEIR · NAMES · BE
NOT · FORGOTTEN

CONTENTS

ILLUSTRATIONS

PREFACE

DURING the Great War many old boys of the Glasgow Academy served in the Imperial Forces, and a considerable number of these fell on the Field or died on Service. The late Major Peter Couper, O.B.E., T.D., who was for many years in command of the Officers' Training Corps, undertook the preparation of a Roll of Honour. The first edition of this was published in October 1918 while the War was still in progress. It was of necessity incomplete, but it was published as a nucleus round which might be gathered material for a complete and final edition. Unfortunately, while Major Couper was engaged in collecting the material for this final edition, his health broke down, and his sudden and unexpected death brought the work upon which he was engaged to an abrupt termination.

For some years no steps were taken in the matter, but the Governors of the Academy felt that it was their duty to have this work completed, and in 1929 appointed a Committee for this purpose. The task of revising and completing the Roll, so long after the event, has proved both difficult and protracted. The Committee are conscious that owing to the lapse of time, and the difficulty, in some cases, of tracing relatives, the records are probably incomplete or inaccurate in some respects.

The Roll covers the period from 4th August, 1914, to 11th November, 1918. It contains the names of 1469 former members of the School who served in His Majesty's Forces during the War. Of those who served, 316 fell on the Field or died on Service. In the Upper Gallery of the Academy their names are inscribed on the Memorial Panels, but their real memorial is the School itself under its new endowment. The Governors hope that this simple record of service rendered by Academicals in the Great War will inspire those who come after to cherish the traditions of the School in the spirit of the men who thus served.

G. H. R. LAIRD
Convener
ROLL OF HONOUR COMMITTEE

201 WEST GEORGE STREET
GLASGOW, C. 2
11th November 1933

HONOURS LIST

Victoria Cross - - - - - - - - -	2
Knight Commander of the British Empire - - - -	1
Companion of the Bath - - - - - - -	2
Companion of St. Michael and St. George - - - -	3
Companion of the Star of India - - - - - -	1
Commander of the British Empire - - - - -	2
Distinguished Service Order - - - - - -	18
Bar to Distinguished Service Order - - - - -	1
Distinguished Flying Cross - - - - - -	3
Distinguished Service Cross - - - - - -	2
Officer of the British Empire - - - - - -	12
Military Cross - - - - - - - - -	115
Bars to Military Cross - - - - - - -	12
Member of the British Empire - - - - - -	3
Air Force Cross - - - - - - - -	1
Distinguished Conduct Medal - - - - - -	3
Military Medal - - - - - - - -	4
Foreign Decorations - - - - - - -	31
Mentions in Despatches - - - - - - -	219

FOREIGN DECORATIONS

Legion of Honour - - - - - - - -	2
French War Cross - - - - - - - -	5
French Medal of Honour - - - - - - -	1

Belgian War Cross   -   -   -   -   -   -   -   -   3

Order of the Crown of Italy   -   -   -   -   -   -   3

Order of St. Maurice and St. Lazarus (Italian)   -   -   -   2

Italian War Cross   -   -   -   -   -   -   -   -   2

Order of the Nile (Egyptian)   -   -   -   -   -   -   3

Order of the White Eagle (Serbian)   -   -   -   -   -   1

Order of St. Sava (Serbian)   -   -   -   -   -   -   -   1

Order of the Redeemer (Greek)   -   -   -   -   -   -   1

Hellenic War Cross (Greek)   -   -   -   -   -   -   1

Order of St. Anne (Russian)   -   -   -   -   -   -   2

Order of St. Stanislas (Russian)   -   -   -   -   -   -   1

Order of the Star of Nepal   -   -   -   -   -   -   -   1

Order of El Nahda (Hedjaz)   -   -   -   -   -   -   1

Order of the Lion and the Sun (Persian)   -   -   -   -   1

ROLL OF HONOUR

Name	Rank — At beginning of War or on joining	Rank — At end of War	Unit	Casualties	Honours or Decorations	Field of Service
ABRAM, Robert Kerr	Private	Lieutenant	8th Battn. Argyll & Sutherland Highlanders, attached Royal Air Force	Wounded, 4th May, 1917	—	France and Belgium
ADAMS, David Rutherford, M.D.	Lieutenant	Captain	Royal Army Medical Corps	Invalided, 1918	—	Salonika, 1916–1917; Italy, 1917–1918
ADAMS, Hamish B.	Gunner	Lieutenant	Royal Field Artillery	—	—	France, 1917 and 1918
ADAMS, William	Private	Private	Royal Army Medical Corps	—	—	Gallipoli, 1915; Egypt and Palestine, 1915–1918
ADAMSON, David T.	Cadet	Cadet	Glasgow University Officers Training Corps	—	—	France, 1918; Home Service
ADAMSON, John William Mackie	2nd Lieutenant	Lieutenant	Royal Army Service Corps	—	—	—
AITKEN, James	Private	Lieutenant	6th Battn. Highland Light Infantry	Invalided, 1916	—	Gallipoli, 1915–1916; Egypt and Palestine, 1915–1918
AITKEN, James Douglas	2nd Lieutenant	2nd Lieutenant	The Middlesex Regiment	—	—	—
AITKEN, John Boyd	Gunner	2nd Lieutenant	Royal Field Artillery	—	—	—
AITKEN, Mark	Surgeon	Staff Surgeon	Royal Navy	—	—	North Sea, Mediterranean, Black Sea, 1914-1918
ALEXANDER, Arthur Munro	Lieutenant	Captain	5th Battn. The Cameronians (Scottish Rifles)	—	Mentioned in Despatches	France, 1914–15 and 1917

Name.	Rank. At beginning of War or on joining.	Rank. At end of War.	Unit.	Casualties.	Honours or Decorations.	Field of Service.
ALEXANDER, Donald	Cadet	2nd Lieutenant	Cambridge University Officers Training Corps Seaforth Highlanders	—	—	—
ALEXANDER, Douglas E. F.	Despatch rider	Sapper	Royal Engineers	—	—	Italy, 1918
ALEXANDER, George Morgan	Private	Lieutenant	Royal Garrison Artillery	—	—	Home Service
ALEXANDER, Gilchrist	Captain	Captain	General List	—	—	Home Service
ALEXANDER, James Browning	Lieutenant	Major	Royal Army Medical Corps	—	—	France, 1915–1918
ALEXANDER, John Charles	2nd Lieutenant	Lieutenant	Royal Artillery	—	—	France, 1918
ALEXANDER, Ronald Ross	2nd Lieutenant	Major	Royal Field Artillery	Invalided, December 1915	Military Cross	France, 1915
ALEXANDER, Turnbull Clark	Private	Lieutenant	9th (G.H.) Battn. Highland Light Infantry	—	Mentioned in Despatches	France, 1914–1918
ALEXANDER, Sir William	Captain	Brigadier-General	6th Battn. The Black Watch (Royal Highlanders)	—	Mentioned in Despatches twice Distinguished Service Order Companion of the Order of St. Michael and St. George	France, 1915–1916

Name	Rank — At beginning of War or on joining	Rank — At end of War	Unit	Casualties	Honours or Decorations	Field of Service
ALEXANDER, Sir William *Continued*					Companion of the Order of the Bath Knight Commander of the Order of the British Empire Legion of Honour 5th Class Order of St. Maurice and St. Lazarus 4th Class	
ALEXANDER, William	Pioneer	Pioneer	Royal Engineers	—	—	France, 1917–1918
✠ ALEXANDER, William Fairlie	Private	Lieutenant	9th (G.H.) Battn. Highland Light Infantry	Wounded, 1916 Wounded, March 1918 Killed in action, 12th October, 1918, at Le Cateau	—	France, 1914–1918
✠ ALEXANDER, William Mercer	Private	2nd. Lieutenant	17th Battn. Highland Light Infantry	Killed in action, 1st July, 1916, at Thiepval	—	France, 1916
ALLAN, Alexander Robert	2nd Lieutenant	Lieutenant	8th Battn. Argyll & Sutherland Highlanders	—	—	France, 1917
✠ ALLAN, George Waldo	Private	Private	9th (G.H.) Battn. Highland Light Infantry	Killed in action, 17th May, 1915	—	France, 1914–1915
ALLAN, Malcolm A.	Cadet	2nd Lieutenant	10th Officer Cadet Battn.	—	—	Home Service
ALLAN, Maitland	2nd Lieutenant	2nd Lieutenant	Royal Air Force	—	—	—

NAME.	RANK. At beginning of War or on joining.	RANK. At end of War.	UNIT.	CASUALTIES.	HONOURS OR DECORATIONS.	FIELD OF SERVICE.
ALLAN, Ronald James	Private	Captain	The Cameronians (Scottish Rifles) Indian Army	Wounded	Military Cross	Mediterranean Expeditionary Force, 1915 Egypt and Palestine, 1916-1918
✠ ALLAN, Ramsay	Pilot	2nd Lieutenant	Royal Air Force	Wounded Killed in action	—	France
ANDERSON, A. Harvie	Major	Major	Royal Engineers	—	—	—
ANDERSON, Adam Kelly	Private	Private	Highland Light Infantry	—	—	—
✠ ANDERSON, Alexander Ronald	Private	2nd Lieutenant	1st Battn. Highland Light Infantry	Killed in action, 8th October, 1915, near Vieille-Chapelle	—	France, 1914-1915
✠ ANDERSON, Andrew Douglas McArthur	2nd Lieutenant	Lieutenant	9th Battn. Argyll & Sutherland Highlanders	Killed in action, 8th May, 1915	—	France
✠ ANDERSON, Charles Hamilton	Captain	Captain	Highland Light Infantry	Killed in action, 19th December, 1914, near Givenchy	—	India and France
ANDERSON, David Blythe	Lieut-Commander	Lieut-Commander	Royal Naval Volunteer Reserve	—	—	—
ANDERSON, Harold Scott	Private	2nd Lieutenant	The Cameronians (Scottish Rifles) Royal Field Artillery	—	—	—

NAME.	RANK. At beginning of War or on joining.	RANK. At end of War.	UNIT.	CASUALTIES.	HONOURS OR DECORATIONS.	FIELD OF SERVICE.
ANDERSON, Ian F. L.	2nd Lieutenant	Lieutenant	Argyll & Sutherland Highlanders 7th Battn. Seaforth Highlanders	Wounded, 21st October, 1918	—	France, 1918
✠ ANDERSON, James Kirkwood	2nd Lieutenant	Captain	7th Battn. The Cameronians (Scottish Rifles)	Died of Wounds received 24th November, 1917	—	Gallipoli 1915, Egypt and Palestine, 1916–1917
ANDERSON, J. Wallace	Captain	Lieut-Colonel	Royal Army Medical Corps	—	—	France, 1917–1918
✠ ANDERSON, Mathew	Lieutenant	Captain	9th (G.H.) Battn. Highland Light Infantry	Killed in action, August 1916 at Delville Wood	—	Flanders 1914–1916
ANDERSON, R. Eric	2nd Lieutenant	Lieutenant	Royal Field Artillery	—	—	—
ANDERSON, T. A. Harvie	Captain	Major	9th (G.H.) Battn. Highland Light Infantry Secretary, Glasgow Territorial Force Association		Companion of the Order of the Bath	Home Service
✠ ANDERSON, William Herbert	Captain	Lieut.-Colonel	12th Battn. Highland Light Infantry	Killed in action, 25th March, 1918, near Maricourt	Mentioned in Despatches Victoria Cross	France, 1914–1918
ANDREW, Charles Wood	Private	Major	9th (G.H.) Battn. Highland Light Infantry Royal Field Artillery	Wounded, Somme, 1916, Arras 1917, Ypres 1918	Mentioned in Despatches three times Military Cross Bar to Military Cross	France, 1914–1918

NAME.	RANK. At beginning of War or on joining.	RANK. At end of War.	UNIT.	CASUALTIES.	HONOURS OR DECORATIONS.	FIELD OF SERVICE.
ANDREW, William Monro	2nd Lieutenant	Lieutenant	9th (G.H.) Battn. Highland Light Infantry	Wounded and prisoner of war, 20th May, 1917	—	France, 1916–1917
ANDREWS, C. W.	Lieutenant	Captain	Highland Light Infantry	—	—	—
ANNAN, Thomas Craig	Private	Captain	5th Battn. The Cameronians (Scottish Rifles) 14th Battn. Argyll and Sutherland Highlanders Royal Air Force	—	Distinguished Flying Cross	France, 1914–1918
ARBUCKLE, David Whitelaw	Sergeant	Lieutenant	5th Battn. Queens Own Cameron Highlanders	Wounded twice 1915 Gassed, 1916	—	France, 1915–1916
ARMOUR, James	Private	Private	Royal Army Service Corps	—	—	Mesopotamia, 1917–1918 Palestine, 1918
ARMOUR, William N. M.	Private	Lieutenant	16th Battn. Highland Light Infantry	Invalided, 2nd June, 1917	—	France, 1916–1917
ARROL, A. Theodore	Captain	Captain	9th Battn. Argyll & Sutherland Highlanders	Wounded, Ypres, 1915 Wounded, Lys, 1918	Military Cross,	France and Flanders, 1915–1918
ARTHUR, Charles F.	Private	Lieutenant	Highland Light Infantry Royal Air Force	—	—	—
ARTHUR, Charles Gordon	2nd Lieutenant	Major	Calcutta Light Horse Royal Field Artillery	Invalided, August 1916	Military Cross,	India, 1914 India, Egypt, France, 1915 France, 1916–1918
ARTHUR, David Sloan	Captain	Major	8th Battn. The Cameronians (Scottish Rifles)	Wounded, September 1917 Invalided, November 1918	Military Cross	France, 1917–1918

NAME.	RANK. At beginning of War or on joining.	RANK. At end of War.	UNIT.	CASUALTIES.	HONOURS OR DECORATIONS.	FIELD OF SERVICE.
ARTHUR, John William	Captain	Captain	Labour Corps	—	Mentioned in Despatches	German East Africa, 1917–1918
✠ ARTHUR, W. Ronald	Private	Private	8th Battn. Argyll & Sutherland Highlanders	Killed in action, 13th November, 1916, at Beaumont Hamel	—	France, 1916
ASPIN, James	Private	Cadet	Royal Army Service Corps Royal Air Force	Wounded, May 1918	—	France, 1917–1918
AYLES, Carrington Nunn	Lance-Corporal	Lance-Corporal	Royal Army Medical Corps	—	—	—
BACON, Eric T. G.	Cadet	Private	Officer Cadet Battalion The Cameronians (Scottish Rifles)	—	—	—
BACON, Henry Ernest Cyril	2nd Lieutenant	Major	The Cameronians (Scottish Rifles)	—	Military Cross	France, 1914–1918
BACON, Lionel P. S.	2nd Lieutenant	Lieutenant	Royal Field Artillery	—	—	—
BAIRD, Alexander	Private	2nd Lieutenant	3rd Battn. Argyll & Sutherland Highlanders 6th Battn. The Cameronians (Scottish Rifles)	—	—	Egypt, 1918 Belgium, 1918
BAIRD, James	Surgeon-Probationer	Surgeon-Probationer	Royal Naval Volunteer Reserve	—	—	North Sea, 1916–1918

NAME.	RANK. At beginning of War or on joining.	RANK. At end of War.	UNIT.	CASUALTIES.	HONOURS OR DECORATIONS.	FIELD OF SERVICE.
BAIRD, John F.	Cadet	Sergeant	Glasgow University Officers Training Corps	—	—	Home Service
BAIRD-SMITH, Frank	Private	Captain	5th Battn. The Cameronians (Scottish Rifles)	Wounded, September 1915	Military Cross	France, 1914-1915, 1916-1918
✠ BAIRD-SMITH, James Geddes	Private	Private	24th Battn. The Royal Fusiliers (2nd Sportsmans)	Killed in action, 5th February, 1916	—	France, 1915-1916
BALDERSTON, James	Lieutenant	Lieutenant	The King's Royal Rifle Corps	Invalided, December 1918	—	Salonika, 1917-1918
BALDERSTON, W. Fife	Private	Captain	9th (G.H.) Battn. Highland Light Infantry	—	Mentioned in Despatches	France, 1914-1916, 1917-1918
BALFOUR, John	Lieutenant-Colonel	Lieutenant-Colonel	Royal Scots Fusiliers	Invalided	—	—
✠ BALLINGAL, John Rennie	Private	Private	Canadian Infantry	Killed in action, 9th January, 1917	—	France
BAMFORD, Cyril Assafrey	Midshipman	Sub-Lieutenant	Royal Navy	—	Distinguished Service Cross	North Sea, 1915-1916; Devonport Defence Flotilla, 1917; Salonika, 1917; Adriatic, 1918; Grand Fleet, 1918
BAPTIE, John W. A.	2nd Lieutenant	2nd Lieutenant	Highland Light Infantry	—	—	—

Name.	Rank. At beginning of War or on joining.	Rank. At end of War.	Unit.	Casualties.	Honours or Decorations.	Field of Service.
✠ Barbé, Adrien E.	Private	Lieutenant	9th (G.H.) Battn. Highland Light Infantry Royal Air Force	Drowned by sinking of transport, 27th May, 1918	—	France
Barbé, Louis Allen	Trooper	Captain	Ayrshire Yeomanry Highland Light Infantry Royal Flying Corps Royal Air Force	—	—	—
Barbour, Archibald Robertson	Private	Captain	Royal Field Artillery	—	Mentioned in Despatches Officer of the Order of the British Empire	East Africa, 1914-1918
Barclay, George	Chaplain	Chaplain	Royal Army Chaplains Department	—	—	France, 1915-1918
✠ Barr, Frederick Train	Private	Private	9th (G.H.) Battn. Highland Light Infantry	Killed in action, 25th February, 1915	—	France, 1914-1915
✠ Barr, John Lyle	Gunner	Lieutenant	Royal Field Artillery	Died of Wounds, 26th July, 1916	—	France, 1916
Barr, Peter Gray	Trooper	2nd Lieutenant	Queen's Own Royal Glasgow Yeomanry Tank Corps	—	—	—
Barr, Robert	Private	Private	Argyll & Sutherland Highlanders	—	—	—
Barr, Robert Irwin	Private	Lieutenant	Royal Army Service Corps	—	—	France, 1916-1918

Name.	Rank. At beginning of War or on joining.	Rank. At end of War.	Unit.	Casualties.	Honours or Decorations.	Field of Service.
✠ BARR, William Speirs	—	Captain	9th (G.H.) Battn. Highland Light Infantry	Died of Wounds, 23rd May, 1917	—	France, 1914–1917
BARRADELL-SMITH, Walter	Private	Lieutenant	28th London Regiment (Artists Rifles) 15th Officer Cadet Battn. The Cameronians (Scottish Rifles)	—	—	France, 1918
✠ BARRAS, William	Private	2nd Lieutenant	8th Battn. Argyll & Sutherland Highlanders	Died of wounds, 21st March, 1918	Military Medal	France, 1915–1918
BATTERSBY, James Robert Gloag	Cadet	Cadet	Glasgow University Officers Training Corps	—	—	Home Service
BAXTER, Alexander R.	2nd Lieutenant	Lieutenant	Argyll & Sutherland Highlanders	—	—	—
BAYNE, A. M.	Major	Major	Royal Field Artillery	—	—	—
BAYNE, Charles Malloch	Captain	Lieut-Colonel	Royal Field Artillery	Wounded, 1915	Mentioned in Despatches	Gallipoli, 1915–1916 France, 1916–1918
BEATTIE, William	2nd Lieutenant	2nd Lieutenant	Glasgow Yeomanry	—	—	—
BECKETT, Alexander Oliphant	2nd Lieutenant	Lieutenant	5th Battn. Highland Light Infantry Royal Flying Corps	—	—	France, 1917

Name.	Rank. At beginning of War or on joining.	Rank. At end of War.	Unit.	Casualties.	Honours or Decorations.	Field of Service.
BECKETT, Henry Paul	Trooper	Lieutenant	Queen's Own Royal Glasgow Yeomanry	Invalided, 1915 and 1918	—	Gallipoli, 1915; Egypt and Palestine, 1916–1918
BECKETT, William	Lieutenant	Captain	5th Battn. Highland Light Infantry	Invalided, September 1915	Mentioned in Despatches twice; Silver Medal of Crown of Italy	Gallipoli, 1915; Egypt and Palestine, 1915–1918
✠ BEGG, Alexander James	Lieutenant	Lieutenant	17th Battn. Highland Light Infantry	Wounded, April 1916; Wounded, 1st July, 1916 and died, 9th July, 1916	Mentioned in Despatches; Military Cross	France, 1915–1916
BEGG, David Henderson	Private	Captain	8th Battn. The Cameronians (Scottish Rifles)	Wounded, January 1917	Mentioned in Despatches	Egypt and Sinai Peninsula, 1916; Mesopotamia, 1916–1918
BEGG, George Douglas	Captain	Captain	Royal Scots Fusiliers	Wounded, September 1915 and May 1917	Mentioned in Despatches twice; Military Cross	France, 1915
BEGG, James M.	Lieut-Commander	Captain	Royal Navy	—	Mentioned in Despatches	North America and West Indies Station, 1914–1915; Dardanelles, 1915; Grand Fleet, 1916–1917
BEGG, Robert Alexander	Lieutenant	Captain	7th Battn. Seaforth Highlanders	Wounded, September 1915; Gassed, March 1918; Prisoner of War, 1918	—	France, 1915, 1917–1918
BEGG, Robert William	2nd Lieutenant	Captain	5th Battn. The Cameronians (Scottish Rifles)	—	—	France, 1914–1915, 1917–1918

NAME.	RANK. At beginning of War or on joining.	RANK. At end of War.	UNIT.	CASUALTIES.	HONOURS OR DECORATIONS.	FIELD OF SERVICE.
BELL, Frederic A.	Captain	Captain	Royal Engineers	—	Mentioned in Despatches twice, Military Cross	Egypt, 1915–1916, France, 1916–1918
BELL, Robert	Cadet	Cadet	Glasgow University Officers Training Corps	—	—	Home Service
BELL, Robert C.	Private	Private	Royal Army Service Corps	—	—	—
✝ BENNETT, William Munro	2nd Lieutenant	Lieutenant	8th Battn. Argyll & Sutherland Highlanders	Died of wounds received in action, 18th June, 1916	—	France, 1915–1916
✝ BENZIE, William Gardner	Private	2nd Lieutenant	7th Battn. Canadian Infantry	Died of wounds, 10th April, 1917	—	France, 1915–1917
BESTER, Louis	Private	Private	Argyll & Sutherland Highlanders	—	—	—
BIGGART, J. A.	Cadet	2nd Lieutenant	10th Officer Cadet Battn. Gordon Highlanders	—	—	Home Service
BILSLAND A. Steven	2nd Lieutenant	Captain	8th Battn. The Cameronians (Scottish Rifles)	—	Military Cross	Egypt and Palestine, 1916–1918, France, 1918
BILSLAND, James A.	2nd Lieutenant	Lieutenant	Royal Engineers	—	—	France, 1918
BINNIE, J. A. W.	Private	Captain	17th Battn. Highland Light Infantry, 5th Battn. Highland Light Infantry, Royal Air Force	—	—	France, 1917

NAME.	RANK. At beginning of War or on joining.	RANK. At end of War.	UNIT.	CASUALTIES.	HONOURS OR DECORATIONS.	FIELD OF SERVICE.
✠ BINNIE, David Willis	Private	2nd. Lieutenant	17th Battn. Highland Light Infantry	Killed in action, 27th May, 1917	—	France, 1917
✠ BINNING, Robert Inglis	Captain	Captain	Indian Medical Service	Died on service, 16th August, 1916	—	Mesopotamia, 1916
BIRD, Neilson Moore	Midshipman	Lieutenant	Royal Navy	—	—	North Sea, 1915-1918
BIRD, Wilfred J.	Officer British Red Cross Society	Officer British Red Cross Society	British Red Cross Society Friends Ambulance Unit	—	—	Belgium, 1914-1918
BIRRELL, Alexander	Lieut-Colonel	Lieut-Colonel	5th Battn. Highland Light Infantry	—	—	—
BIRRELL, R. Campbell	Private	Private	Australian Imperial Forces	Discharged medically unfit	—	Home Service
✠ BIRRELL, William Henry	Bombardier	2nd. Lieutenant	Bute Mountain Battery, 8th Battn. The Cameronians (Scottish Rifles)	Killed in action, 20th September, 1918	—	Salonika, 1917-1918
✠ BLACK, Arthur Bloomfield	Private	2nd. Lieutenant	Royal Army Medical Corps	Invalided, January 1918 Died from effects of active service	—	France, 1915-1918
BLACK, Colin Charteris	Lieutenant	Lieutenant	Queen's Own Royal Glasgow Yeomanry	—	—	France, 1916-1918

NAME.	RANK. At beginning of War or on joining.	RANK. At end of War.	UNIT.	CASUALTIES.	HONOURS OR DECORATIONS.	FIELD OF SERVICE.
BLACK, Douglas Honeyman	Private	2nd Lieutenant	Royal Garrison Artillery	—	—	Home Service
BLACK, Howard Charteris	2nd Lieutenant	Flight-Lieutenant	Highland Light Infantry Royal Flying Corps Royal Air Force	—	—	France, 1916–1918
BLACK, Robert Greenhill	Captain	Captain	Indian Army	Invalided, December 1918	—	France, 1917–1918 Kuki-Chin Expedition, 1918
✠ BLACK, William	Chaplain (Fourth Class)	Chaplain (Fourth Class)	Royal Army Chaplains Department	Invalided Died, 10th July, 1918, at Boulogne	—	France, 1918
BLAKELY, Gordon Wilson	Private	Private	9th (G.H.) Battn. Highland Light Infantry	Wounded, September 1915 Wounded, May 1916 Wounded, September 1917	—	France, 1915–1917
✠ BLAKELY, John Douglas	2nd. Lieutenant	2nd Lieutenant	9th Battn. Gordon Highlanders	Killed in action, 9th April, 1917, at Arras	—	France, 1916–1917
BLAKELY, John Houghton	Gunner	Fitter Staff Sergeant	Royal Field Artillery	Wounded and Invalided, March 1918	Mentioned in Despatches	France, 1915–1918
BLYTH, Robert Oswald	2nd Lieutenant	Lieutenant	Royal Garrison Artillery	—	—	Home Service
BOCK, Arthur Francis	Private	Captain	6th Battn. The Manchester Regiment	—	—	Egypt, 1914–1915 German East Africa, 1916–1918

NAME.	RANK. At beginning of War or on joining.	RANK. At end of War.	UNIT.	CASUALTIES.	HONOURS OR DECORATIONS.	FIELD OF SERVICE.
BOCK, John Ralston	Captain	Lieut-Colonel	9th (G.H.) Battn. Highland Light Infantry	Wounded, September 1916	Mentioned in Despatches	France, 1914–1916 and 1918
✠ BONNAR, James Crawford	2nd Lieutenant	Lieutenant	9th Battn. Argyll & Sutherland Highlanders	Killed on service, May 1915	—	France, 1915
BORLAND, Douglas Morris	Lieutenant	Captain	Royal Army Medical Corps	—	Mentioned in Despatches	France, 1914–1915 Salonika, 1915–1918
BORLAND, Edward Theodore	Paymaster Sub-Lieutenant	Paymaster Sub-Lieutenant	Royal Naval Reserve	—	—	At Sea, 1917–1918
BORLAND, Julius	Private	2nd Lieutenant	Royal Army Service Corps 8th Battn. The Cameronians (Scottish Rifles)	—	—	France, 1915–1918
BORTHWICK, Walter Greig	2nd Lieutenant	Captain	5th Battn. The Cameronians (Scottish Rifles) 19th Trench Mortar Battery	—	Military Cross	France, 1916–1918
Bow, John Walker	2nd Lieutenant	2nd Lieutenant	The Cameronians (Scottish Rifles)	—	—	—
Bow, William S.	Lieutenant	Captain	6th Battn. The Cameronians (Scottish Rifles)	—	—	Egypt and France, 1917–1918
BOYD, Alexander Davie	2nd Lieutenant	2nd Lieutenant	Argyll & Sutherland Highlanders	—	—	—

Name.	Rank. At beginning of War or on joining.	Rank. At end of War.	Unit.	Casualties.	Honours or Decorations.	Field of Service.
Boyd, Edward R.	2nd Lieutenant	Captain	8th Battn. The Cameronians (Scottish Rifles)	—	—	—
Boyd, Gavin	Lieutenant	Lieutenant	Argyll & Sutherland Highlanders	—	—	—
Boyd, James	Captain	Lieut-Colonel	6th Battn. The Cameronians (Scottish Rifles)	Wounded, May 1915. Invalided, January 1917–April 1917	—	France, 1915–1918
✠ Boyd, James Milne	Private	Private	The Cameronians (Scottish Rifles)	Killed in action, 21st June, 1917, at Ypres	—	France
✠ Boyd, John	Private	2nd Lieutenant	17th Battn. Highland Light Infantry. 6th Battn. The Cameronians (Scottish Rifles)	Killed in action, 29th October, 1916 —	—	France, 1916
Boyd, John	Private	Private	Gordon Highlanders	—	—	—
✠ Boyd, Reginald R.	2nd Lieutenant	2nd Lieutenant	The Cameronians (Scottish Rifles)	Died of wounds, 4th May, 1917	—	France
Boyd, Ronald	Private	Private	Royal Army Medical Corps	—	—	—
✠ Boyd, William	Private	Lieutenant	17th Battn. Highland Light Infantry. Royal Field Artillery	Killed in action, 24th March, 1918	Military Cross	France, 1916–1918
✠ Boyd, William	Private	Private	Canadian Infantry	Died on service, 7th May, 1916	—	France

EDWIN TEMPLE, M.A., LL.D.,

RECTOR OF THE ACADEMY 1899-1932

Name.	Rank. At beginning of War or on joining.	Rank. At end of War.	Unit.	Casualties.	Honours or Decorations.	Field of Service.
BOYD, William E.	Surgeon-Lieutenant	Surgeon-Lieutenant	Royal Navy	—	—	North Atlantic, West Indies, Canada, Central America, Florida Straits, Bermuda, South America, Cape Verce Islands, 1916–1917; Scapa Flow, North Sea, 1917–1918; Belgium and France, 1918
BOYLE, Allan	2nd Lieutenant	Captain	Royal Field Artillery Royal Air Force	—	Military Cross Air Force Cross	France, 1915–1917
BRAND, David E.	Captain	Major	5th Battn. Highland Light Infantry	Invalided, August 1915–November 1915; Wounded, November 1917	Mentioned in Despatches twice Distinguished Service Order	Gallipoli, 1915; Egypt and Palestine, 1916–1918; France and Belgium, 1918
✠ BRANDER, Alfred Ernest	2nd. Lieutenant	Lieutenant	8th Battn. Argyll & Sutherland Highlanders	Killed, in action, 13th November, 1916, at Beaumont Hamel	—	France, 1916
✠ BRANDER, Robert William	Surgeon-Lieutenant	Surgeon-Lieutenant	Royal Navy	Accidently killed, 1st May, 1918	—	Atlantic Station
BREEZE, John	Private	Lieutenant	7th Battn. The Cameronians (Scottish Rifles)	Wounded, November 1915; Wounded, February 1917	—	Gallipoli, Egypt and Sinai, 1915–1916; France and Belgium, 1917–1918
BROADFOOT, R. Miller	2nd Lieutenant	Lieutenant	6th Battn. Highland Light Infantry	Wounded, December 1916	—	France, 1916 and 1918

Name.	Rank. At beginning of War or on joining.	Rank. At end of War.	Unit.	Casualties.	Honours or Decorations.	Field of Service.
✠ BROADFOOT, William Allison	2nd Lieutenant	2nd Lieutenant	6th Battn. Highland Light Infantry	Killed in action, 12th July, 1915, at Cape Helles	—	Gallipoli, 1915
✠ BRODIE, Douglas Fountaine	Private	Lieutenant	9th (G.H.) Battn. Highland Light Infantry	Gassed, 1916. Killed in action, 12th October, 1918	Mentioned in Despatches. Military Cross	France, 1914–1918
BRODIE, J. Wallace	Lieutenant	Lieutenant	2/6th Royal Jat Light Infantry (Indian Army)	—	—	Burma, 1914–1916. Northern India and Frontier, 1916–1918
BRODIE, R. Hume	Private	Lieutenant	The Royal Scots (Royal Regiment) Seaforth Highlanders	—	—	—
BROUGH, Thomas	2nd Lieutenant	Captain	Royal Field Artillery	Wounded, November 1917 and October 1918	—	France and Belgium, 1917–1918
BROWN, Adam Gillison	Sergeant	2nd Lieutenant	Glasgow University Officers Training Corps. 3rd Battn. Argyll & Sutherland Highlanders	—	—	Home Service
✠ BROWN, Alexander	2nd Lieutenant	2nd Lieutenant	16th Battn. The Royal Scots (Royal Regiment)	Killed in action, 28th April, 1917, at Arras	—	France, 1916–1917
BROWN, Alexander D. Gordon	Private	2nd Lieutenant	Highland Light Infantry	—	—	—
BROWN, A. W.	2nd Lieutenant	2nd Lieutenant	The Cameronians (Scottish Rifles)	—	—	—

NAME.	RANK. At beginning of War or on joining.	RANK. At end of War.	UNIT.	CASUALTIES.	HONOURS OR DECORATIONS.	FIELD OF SERVICE.
BROWN, Andrew	Lieutenant	Lieutenant	6th Battn. Argyll & Sutherland Highlanders	Gassed, November 1917	—	France and Belgium, 1914–1918
✠ BROWN, Arthur Hugh	Private	Captain	South African Scottish	Killed in action, 1916, at Delville Wood	—	German S.W. Africa, 1914–1915 Egypt, 1915 France, 1916
BROWN, C. Arrol	Private	Lieutenant	73rd Battn. Royal Highlanders of Canada Royal Air Force	—	—	France, 1915–1918
✠ BROWN, Douglas Knox	Private	Lieutenant	Queen's Own Cameron Highlanders	Killed in action, 30th November, 1917	Military Cross	France
✠ BROWN, Hugh Alexander	Private	2nd Lieutenant	9th (G.H.) Battn. The Highland Light Infantry 9th Battn. The Cameronians (Scottish Rifles)	Killed in action, 14th July, 1916, at Longueval	—	France, 1915–1916
BROWN, Jaime C.	2nd Lieutenant	2nd Lieutenant	Argyll & Sutherland Highlanders	—	—	—
BROWN, James Archibald	Captain	Major	Calcutta Scottish	—	—	India
✠ BROWN, James Archibald Macmillan	Private	Private	5th Battn. Queen's Own Cameron Highlanders	Killed in action, 27th September, 1915, at Loos	—	France, 1915
✠ BROWN, James Hardie	2nd Lieutenant	Captain	6th Battn. Argyll & Sutherland Highlanders	Killed in action, 7th July, 1918	Military Cross	France and Italy

Name.	Rank. At beginning of War or on joining.	Rank. At end of War.	Unit.	Casualties.	Honours or Decorations.	Field of Service.
✠ Brown, James William	Lieutenant	Captain	The Royal Scots (Royal Regiment)	Wounded, June 1915, 21st Killed in action, March, 1917	Military Cross	France, 1915–1917
Brown, John M.	Private	—	17th Battn. Highland Light Infantry	—	—	Home Service
✠ Brown, Kenneth Ashby	Lieutenant	Captain	5th Battn. The Cameronians (Scottish Rifles)	Invalided, June 1914, 14th Killed in action, April, 1917, at Arras	Mentioned in Despatches	France, 1915–1917
Brown, Ralph S. Stark	Private	Captain (Flight Commander)	9th (G.H.) Battn. Highland Light Infantry Royal Air Force	Wounded, January 1918	Military Cross	France, 1915–1918
Brown, Robert Archibald	Surgeon-Lieutenant	Surgeon-Lieutenant	Royal Navy	—	—	At Sea, 1914–1916 Royal Naval Hospital, South Queensferry, 1916–1918
Brown, Robert Louis	Sub-Lieutenant	Sub-Lieutenant	Royal Naval Air Service	Wounded	—	—
Brown, Robert R.	2nd Lieutenant	2nd Lieutenant	Highland Light Infantry	—	—	—
Brown, Robert Robertson	Private	Lieutenant	2nd Battn. Highland Light Infantry	—	Mentioned in Despatches	France, 1916–1918
✠ Brown, Robert Stanley	2nd Lieutenant	2nd Lieutenant	16th Battn. Highland Light Infantry	Killed in action, 1st July, 1916	—	France, 1915–1916

Name.	Rank. At beginning of War or on joining.	Rank. At end of War.	Unit.	Casualties.	Honours or Decorations.	Field of Service.
Brown, Thomas D. S.	2nd Lieutenant	Lieutenant	7th Battn The Cameronians (Scottish Rifles)	—	—	West Africa, 1915–1917
Brown, Tom Cunningham	Corporal	Corporal	Lovat Scouts	—	—	Suvla Bay, Egypt, Sinai Peninsula, Salonika and France, 1915
✠ Brown, W. Fraser	Sub-Lieutenant	Lieutenant	Royal Naval Volunteer Reserve	Killed in action, 7th June, 1915, at Gallipoli	—	Gallipoli, 1915
Brown, William Archibald Scott	Lance-Corporal	Flight-Lieutenant	Northern Cyclist Battalion Royal Air Force	Prisoner of War, 1916	—	France, 1915–1916
Browning, Archibald	Private	Captain	6th Battn. The Royal Fusiliers (City of London Regiment)	Wounded, April 1917	—	France, 1915–1917
✠ Brownlie, John Reid	Private	2nd Lieutenant	11th Battn. The Cameronians (Scottish Rifles)	Killed in action, 29th June, 1916	—	France, 1915–1916
Bryce, Henry S.	Private	Private	The Black Watch (Royal Highlanders)	—	—	—
Bryce, John	Private	Cadet	Royal Scots Fusiliers Royal Air Force	—	—	—
Buchanan, Duncan Archibald	Lieutenant	Lieutenant	8th Battn. The Cameronians (Scottish Rifles)	Wounded and Invalided, March 1918	—	France, 1917–1918
Buchanan, Eric C.	2nd Lieutenant	Captain	7th (Blythswood) Battn. Highland Light Infantry	Invalided, September 1915	—	Gallipoli, 1915

NAME.	RANK. At beginning of War or on joining.	RANK. At end of War.	UNIT.	CASUALTIES.	HONOURS OR DECORATIONS.	FIELD OF SERVICE.
BUCHANAN, Hector	Private	2nd Lieutenant	5th Battn. Queen's Own Cameron Highlanders	Invalided, December 1917	—	France, 1915
BUCHANAN, William L.	Gunner	Gunner	Royal Field Artillery	—	—	Home Service
✠ BUCHANAN, William Learmonth	Lieutenant	Captain	5th Battn. Highland Light Infantry	Died of wounds, 20th November, 1917	—	Egypt, Gallipoli, and Palestine, 1915-1917
BUCHANAN, William Lister	Cadet	Signaller	Edinburgh University Officers Training Corps Royal Field Artillery	—	—	—
BURRELL, Gordon	Private	Private	Highland Light Infantry	—	—	—
BURRELL, Thomas MacKaig	Private	Captain	9th (G.H.) Battn. Highland Light Infantry	—	—	East Africa, 1917-1918
✠ BURRELL, William	Lieutenant	Lieutenant	Royal Naval Volunteer Reserve	Accidentally drowned, 18th November, 1914	—	North Sea
BURTON, James Wilson	Lieutenant	Captain	Royal Army Medical Corps	Wounded twice	—	Gallipoli, Egypt, Palestine, France and India
BURTON, Thomas Menzies	Private	Lieutenant	9th (G.H.) Battn. Highland Light Infantry	Wounded, July 1916 Wounded, August 1916 Invalided, January 1917	Mentioned in Despatches Military Cross	France, 1914-1916
BURTON, William M. Wilson	2nd Lieutenant	Lieutenant	Royal Engineers	—	—	—

Name	Rank (At beginning of War or on joining)	Rank (At end of War)	Unit	Casualties	Honours or Decorations	Field of Service
Bush, Cecil F.	Gunner	2nd Lieutenant	Royal Field Artillery	—	—	Home Service
Cairney, William	Private	Corporal	Queen's Own Cameron Highlanders	Invalided	—	—
Cairns, Robert	3rd Air Mechanic	3rd Air Mechanic	Royal Air Force	—	—	—
Cairns, Thomas Munro	Sergeant	Sergeant	Royal Engineers, Canadian Forces	—	—	—
Caldwell, James	Lieutenant	Lieutenant	3rd Battn. Argyll & Sutherland Highlanders	—	—	France and Belgium, 1918
Caldwell, Robert Stevenson	Surgeon-Sub-Lieutenant	Surgeon-Sub-Lieutenant	Royal Naval Volunteer Reserve	Invalided, May 1917	—	Active Service abroad, 1914–1917
✠ Caldwell, Stewart	Private	2nd Lieutenant	Royal Air Force	Died, November 1918	—	Home Service
Caldwell, William Abercrombie	Private	Cadet Corporal	Edinburgh University Officers Training Corps	—	—	Home Service
Cameron, Alexander Duncan	Lieutenant	Major	8th Battn. The Cameronians (Scottish Rifles)	Invalided, 1918	Member of the Order of the British Empire	France, 1916–1918
✠ Cameron, Donald R. C.	2nd Lieutenant	Lieutenant	11th Battn. Highland Light Infantry	Killed in action, 13th September, 1915	—	France, 1915

Name.	Rank. At beginning of War or on joining.	Rank. At end of War.	Unit.	Casualties.	Honours or Decorations.	Field of Service.
CAMERON, William Moore	2nd Lieutenant	Captain	Royal Army Medical Corps	Wounded, June 1918	Mentioned in Despatches three times)	France, 1917; Mesopotamia, 1917; Palestine, 1917–1918
CAMERON, William Norman	Cadet	2nd Lieutenant	Glasgow University Officers Training Corps; Argyll & Sutherland Highlanders Machine Gun Corps Tank Corps	Wounded	—	—
CAMPBELL, Charles Arthur	2nd Lieutenant	2nd Lieutenant	10th Battn. The Border Regiment	Invalided, June 1916	—	Egypt, 1916
CAMPBELL, Finlay Stewart	2nd Lieutenant	Captain	Royal Army Medical Corps	—	—	Home Service
✠ CAMPBELL, Glenlyon Archibald	Lieutenant-Colonel	Lieutenant-Colonel	107th Battn. Canadian Pioneers	Died, 23rd October, 1917, at Etaples	Mentioned in Despatches Distinguished Service Order	France, 1917
CAMPBELL, Gordon	Cadet	Cadet	Glasgow University Officers Training Corps	—	—	Home Service
CAMPBELL, James C.	Major	Major	5th Battn. The Cameronians (Scottish Rifles)	Invalided, May 1915	—	France, 1914–1915
CAMPBELL, John J.	Cadet	Cadet	Glasgow University Officers Training Corps	—	—	Home Service

NAME.	RANK. At beginning of War or on joining.	RANK. At end of War.	UNIT.	CASUALTIES.	HONOURS OR DECORATIONS.	FIELD OF SERVICE.
✠ CAMPBELL, Quentin Hewes	Lieutenant	Captain	King's Own Yorkshire Light Infantry	Killed in action, 19th July, 1917	Military Cross	France
CANDLISH, James	Gunner	Corporal	Motor Machine Gun Corps	—	—	France, 1916–1918
✠ CANDLISH, William Gordon	Private	Private	Argyll & Sutherland Highlanders	Wounded and missing, 24th August, 1917	—	France
CARGILL, William A.	Lieutenant	Lieutenant	Royal Engineers	Wounded, April 1918	—	France, 1917–1918
✠ CARPENTER, John Neilson	Private	2nd Lieutenant	17th Battn. Highland Light Infantry	Killed in action, 1st July, 1916	Military Cross	France, 1915–1916
CARR, Francis T. F.	Lieutenant	Major	5th Battn. The Cameronians (Scottish Rifles)	Wounded, April 1916	Mentioned in Despatches three times Officer of the Order of the British Empire	France, 1916–1918
✠ CARRUTHERS, Donald Ross	Private	Private	9th (G.H.) Battn. Highland Light Infantry	Killed in action, at Loos, 25th September, 1915	—	France
✠ CARRUTHERS, Frank Walter	Private	Private	9th (G.H.) Battn. Highland Light Infantry	Killed in action, 17th May, 1915	—	France, 1914–1915
CARSLAW, Frank H.	Captain	Captain	2nd Surmah Valley Light Horse	—	—	India, 1914–1918
✠ CARSLAW, John Howie	Lieutenant	Lieutenant	Royal Field Artillery	Died of wounds, 26th November, 1917	—	Dardanelles, Egypt and Palestine, 1915–1917

Name.	Rank. At beginning of War or on joining.	Rank. At end of War.	Unit.	Casualties.	Honours or Decorations.	Field of Service.
CARSLAW, Robert B.	Lieutenant	Major	Royal Army Medical Corps	Invalided, 1918	—	France, 1917–1918
CARSLAW, Ronald McGregor	Bombardier	Bombardier	Edinburgh University Officers Training Corps	—	—	Home Service
CARSLAW, William Henderson	2nd Lieutenant	Captain	8th Battn. The Cameronians (Scottish Rifles)	Invalided, September 1915; Wounded, August 1916; Wounded, April 1917	—	Gallipoli, 1915, Sinai and Palestine, 1916–1918
✠ CARSON, Frederick Glover	2nd Lieutenant	2nd Lieutenant	1st Battn. King's Own Scottish Borderers	Killed in action, 30th November, 1917	—	France, 1917
CARSON, John	Trooper	Sergeant	Australian Light Horse	—	—	—
CARSON, William L.	Private	Corporal	Australian Infantry	Wounded	—	—
✠ CARSWELL, John Jamieson	2nd Lieutenant	2nd Lieutenant	10th Battn. The Cameronians (Scottish Rifles)	Killed in action, 25th/27th September, 1915, at Loos	—	France, 1915
CASSELLS, John	Private	Private	Highland Light Infantry	—	—	—
CASSILS, Charles	Midshipman	Lieutenant	Royal Naval Volunteer Reserve	—	—	British West Indies, 1916–1918
✠ CHALMERS, Henry Stewart	2nd Lieutenant	Captain	Royal Field Artillery	Died of wounds, 29th September, 1917	—	Egypt
CHALMERS, Hugh D. D.	Lieut-Colonel	Colonel	6th Battn, Highland Light Infantry	—	Mentioned in Despatches twice	Home Service

NAME.	RANK. At beginning of War or on joining.	RANK. At end of War.	UNIT.	CASUALTIES.	HONORS OR DECORATIONS.	FIELD OF SERVICE.
CHALMERS, W. Kerr	2nd Lieutenant	Major	Royal Field Artillery	Wounded, November 1917	—	France, 1917
CHALMERS, William S.	Lieutenant	Lieutenant-Commander	Royal Navy	—	Mentioned in Despatches Distinguished Service Cross French War Cross	France, 1914 At Sea, 1915–1918
✠ CHURCH, William Campbell	Lieutenant	Captain	8th Battn. The Cameronians (Scottish Rifles)	Killed in action, 28th June, 1915, at Gallipoli	—	Gallipoli, 1915
✠ CLAASEN, Ernest Leopold	Private	Corporal	6th Battn. Highland Light Infantry Army Cyclist Corps	Invalided, 1915 Died of wounds, 22nd April, 1917, at El Arish	—	Gallipoli, Egypt and Palestine, 1915–1917
CLAASEN, Frederick L.	Private	Corporal	Royal Engineers	Wounded, October 1918	—	France and Belgium, 1918
CLAASEN, Harold R. N. C.	Corporal	Corporal	6th Battn. Highland Light Infantry	Wounded, July 1918 Wounded, August 1918	—	France, 1918
CLARK, Alfred MacKenzie	Captain	Captain	Royal Army Medical Corps	—	Military Cross	France, 1915–1918
CLARK, David J.	Signaller	Signaller	Royal Field Artillery	—	—	France and Belgium, 1917–1918
✠ CLARK, Jasper	2nd Lieutenant	Captain	10th Battn. Argyll & Sutherland Highlanders	Killed in action, 2nd October, 1918	—	France 1918

Name.	Rank. At beginning of War or on joining.	Rank. At end of War.	Unit.	Casualties.	Honours or Decorations.	Field of Service.
CLARK, John Combe	Trooper	Captain	Queen's Own Royal Glasgow Yeomanry	Invalided, July 1917	—	Gallipoli, 1915; Egypt, 1916–1917; France, 1917–1918
CLARK, Rudolph J. C.	2nd Lieutenant	Captain	5th Battn. The Cameronians (Scottish Rifles)	—	—	India, 1917–1918
CLARK, Thomas P. M.	Lieutenant	Lieutenant	5th Battn. The Cameronians (Scottish Rifles)	Invalided, March 1918	—	France, 1916
CLARKSON, D. Durward	2nd Lieutenant	Lieutenant	5th Battn. The Cameronians (Scottish Rifles)	Invalided, December 1916	—	France, 1915–1916
CLARKSON, R. Murray	2nd Lieutenant	Captain	Highland Light Infantry Indian Army	Wounded twice	—	—
CLEGHORN, Alexander	2nd Lieutenant	Major	Royal Engineers	Wounded, June 1915	Mentioned in Despatches; Order of the White Eagle of Serbia, 4th Class; Brevet Major	France, 1915; Salonika, 1916–1918; France, 1918
CLEGHORN, William George	Lieutenant	Major	Royal Garrison Artillery Royal Flying Corps Royal Air Force	—	—	France, 1918
CLEMENT, James	Private	Lieutenant	8th Battn. Argyll & Sutherland Highlanders	—	—	France, 1917–1918
CLINK, Charles William	2nd Lieutenant	2nd Lieutenant	The Cameronians (Scottish Rifles)	—	—	—

NAME.	RANK. At beginning of War or on joining.	RANK. At end of War.	UNIT.	HONOURS OR DECORATIONS.	CASUALTIES.	FIELD OF SERVICE.
COATS, Douglas Hamilton	Private	Captain	Royal Army Medical Corps	—	—	India, 1916–1918
COATS, James	Lieutenant-Colonel	Lieutenant-Colonel	Royal Army Medical Corps	—	—	—
COATS, James Walter	Lieutenant	Major	Royal Field Artillery	—	—	Egypt and Palestine, 1916–1918
COATS, John Graham	Captain	Major	9th (G.H.) Battn. Highland Light Infantry	—	—	France, 1914–1915; Palestine, 1918; France, 1918
COATS, Stewart	Captain	Lieut-Colonel	6th Battn. Argyll & Sutherland Highlanders	Mentioned in Despatches twice; Distinguished Service Order	—	France, 1915–1917; Italy, 1917–1918; France, 1918
COATS, Walter John Jackson	Lieutenant	Major	9th (G.H.) Battn. Highland Light Infantry	Mentioned in Despatches; Military Cross	—	France and Flanders, 1914-1918
COATS, Walter William	Chaplain	Chaplain 2nd Class	Royal Army Chaplains Department	—	—	Home Service
COCHRANE, Melville D. M.	Cadet	Cadet	Glasgow University Officers Training Corps	—	—	Home Service
COCKBURN, Harold Andrew	Gunner	Corporal	Royal Field Artillery	—	Invalided, 1917	France and Belgium, 1916–1917

NAME.	RANK. At beginning of War or on joining.	RANK. At end of War.	UNIT.	CASUALTIES.	HONOURS OR DECORATIONS.	FIELD OF SERVICE.
COLLIE, Alexander	Cadet	Cadet	Glasgow University Officers Training Corps	—	—	Home Service
✠ COLQUHOUN, Robert Clark	Private	2nd Lieutenant	9th (G.H.) Battn. Highland Light Infantry 2nd Battn. The Cameronians (Scottish Rifles)	Died of wounds, 3rd July, 1916	—	France, 1914–1916
COLVIL, Harold Campbell	Private	2nd Lieutenant	Highland Light Infantry	—	—	—
COLVIL, J. A. Campbell	Private	Captain	5th Battn. Highland Light Infantry	Invalided, December 1915	—	Gallipoli, 1915
COLVILLE, Arthur J.	Private	Lieutenant	Highland Light Infantry Royal Engineers	Invalided	—	—
CONNAL, James Killoh	Private	Lieutenant	Royal Scots Fusiliers	Wounded, May 1917	—	France, 1915–1917
CONNAL, John	2nd Lieutenant	Captain	3rd Battn. The Cameronians (Scottish Rifles)	Wounded, February 1916	—	France, 1915–1917
CONNAL, Kenneth Hugh Munro	Lieut-Colonel	Lieut-Colonel	Queen's Own Royal Glasgow Yeomanry	—	—	Gallipoli, Egypt, France
✠ CONNELL, Alfred Hamilton	Lieutenant	Captain	2nd Battn. Royal Scots Fusiliers	Killed in action, 28th September, 1915	—	France, 1914–1915
CONNELL, James G.	2nd Lieutenant	Captain	Royal Field Artillery	—	—	France, 1917–1918

Name.	Rank. At beginning of War or on joining.	Rank. At end of War.	Unit.	Casualties.	Honours or Decorations.	Field of Service.
CONNELL, William Kerr	Private	Lieutenant	Highland Light Infantry Royal Army Medical Corps	—	—	—
COOK, Harold	Chief Motor Mechanic	Chief Motor Mechanic	Royal Naval Volunteer Reserve	—	—	Aegean Squadron Base, Mudros, Lemnos, 1918
✠ COOK, Randolph	Private	2nd Lieutenant	9th (G.H.) Battn. Highland Light Infantry 5th Battn. The Cameronians (Scottish Rifles)	Killed in action, 9th April, 1917, at Arras	—	France 1917
COOPER, John Mathieson	2nd Lieutenant	Lieutenant	Royal Engineers	Discharged, March 1918	—	Mudros and Gallipoli, 1915 Salonika, 1916
✠ COOPER, Oliver Henry Donald	Private	Lieutenant	6th Battn. Highland Light Infantry	Killed in action, 8th-9th May, 1917	—	Salonika, 1916–1917
COOPER, Robert Sherriffs	Captain	Captain	Royal Engineers	Wounded, July 1917 Discharged, July 1918	—	Gallipoli, 1915 Egypt and Palestine, 1916–1917
COOPER, William Cooper	Private	Lieutenant	Highland Light Infantry	—	—	Egypt and Palestine, 1917–1918 France, 1918
COPLAND, John L.	Gunner	Gunner	Royal Garrison Artillery	—	—	—
COUPER, P.	Major	Major	Glasgow Academy Officers Training Corps, attached Argyll & Sutherland Highlanders Brigade	—	Officer of the Order of the British Empire	Home Service

NAME.	RANK. At beginning of War or on joining.	RANK. At end of War.	UNIT.	CASUALTIES.	HONOURS OR DECORATIONS.	FIELD OF SERVICE.
COUPER, William A. Scott	Cadet	2nd Lieutenant	Officer Cadet Battalion The Royal Scots (Royal Regiment)	Invalided	—	—
COWIE, Charles Rennie	Private	Lieutenant	Royal Engineers	Invalided, March 1915	—	France and Belgium, 1914–1915
COWIE, Thomas Purdie	Private	Private	Rangoon Volunteer Rifles	—	—	India, 1918
CRABBE, James Lindsay	Motor Car Driver	Motor Car Driver	Young Men's Christian Association	—	—	France
CRADDOCK, Arthur Elmslie Bell	Private	Lieutenant	9th Battn. Argyll & Sutherland Highlanders	Invalided, August 1918	—	France, 1916–1918
CRADDOCK, Lionel Ross	Captain	Captain	Royal Garrison Artillery	Wounded, September 1915 Wounded, August 1918	Military Cross	France, 1915–1918
CRAIG, Archibald	Lieutenant	Major	6th Battn. Argyll & Sutherland Highlanders	Wounded, December 1915	Military Cross	France, 1915–1918
CRAIG, D. Gordon	2nd Lieutenant	2nd Lieutenant	Royal Scots Fusiliers	—	—	—
CRAIG, Hugh James	Private	Captain	9th (G.H.) Battn. Highland Light Infantry	Wounded, February 1915	—	France, 1915–1918
CRAIG, James M.	2nd Lieutenant	2nd Lieutenant	The Border Regiment	—	—	—

NAME.	RANK. At beginning of War or on joining.	RANK. At end of War.	UNIT.	CASUALTIES.	HONOURS OR DECORATIONS.	FIELD OF SERVICE.
CRAIG, Morton	Lieutenant	Captain	15th Battn. Highland Light Infantry	Wounded, November 1916 Invalided, July 1918	—	France, 1915–1916 and 1917–1918
CREIGHTON, Robert	Midshipman	Midshipman	Royal Navy	—	—	—
CRUICKSHANK, John Norman	Captain	Captain	Royal Army Medical Corps	Wounded, September 1916 Wounded, April 1918	Military Cross	France, 1915 and 1916–1918
CUNNINGHAM, A.	Cadet	Bombardier	Edinburgh University Officers Training Corps	—	—	Home Service
✠ CURPHEY, William G. S.	2nd Lieutenant	Captain	Royal Berkshire Regiment Royal Flying Corps	Died of wounds, 15th May, 1917	Military Cross	France
CURRIE, Allan Peter	Private	Captain	9th (G.H.) Battn. Highland Light Infantry	Wounded, May 1915 Wounded, June 1918	Military Cross	France and Belgium, 1914–1915 and 1917–1918
CURRIE, Arthur R.	Private	Cadet	Queen's Own Cameron Highlanders Tank Corps School	—	—	—
✠ CURRIE, Gilbert Heron	Private	2nd Lieutenant	9th (G.H.) Battn. Highland Light Infantry 10th Battn. Argyll & Sutherland Highlanders	Killed in action, 12th October, 1916, on the Somme	Distinguished Conduct Medal	France, 1914–1916
CURRIE, James H.	Lieutenant	Lieutenant	Calcutta Scottish	—	—	—
CURRIE, John	Private	Private	The Cameronians (Scottish Rifles)	—	—	—

c

NAME.	RANK. At beginning of War or on joining.	RANK. At end of War.	UNIT.	CASUALTIES.	HONOURS OR DECORATIONS.	FIELD OF SERVICE.
CURRIE, John H.	2nd Lieutenant	Lieutenant	Trench Mortar Battery	—	—	—
CURRIE, Thomas C.	Cadet	2nd Lieutenant	Glasgow University Officers Training Corps Royal Scots Fusiliers	—	—	—
CURRIE, William Crawford	Corporal	Sergeant	Calcutta Light Horse	—	—	—
CURRIE, William Inglis	Cadet	Cadet	Royal Air Force 28th London Regiment (Artists Rifles)	—	—	Home Service
DAVIDSON, Hamish R.	2nd Lieutenant	Captain	Highland Light Infantry	Invalided, April 1917 Discharged, November 1917	—	France, 1915–1917
✠ DAVIDSON, Henry Steel	2nd Lieutenant	Lieutenant	Highland Light Infantry	Killed in action, 18th May, 1915, at Festubert	—	France, 1915
Davidson, James Noel	Gentleman-Cadet	2nd Lieutenant	Royal Military College, Sandhurst Argyll & Sutherland Highlanders	—	—	—
DAVIDSON, Robert Alexander Murdoch	2nd Lieutenant	2nd Lieutenant	4th Battn. Argyll & Sutherland Highlanders	—	—	Home Service

NAME.	RANK. At beginning of War or on joining.	RANK. At end of War.	UNIT.	CASUALTIES.	HONOURS OR DECORATIONS.	FIELD OF SERVICE.
DAVIDSON, William Cameron	Lieutenant	Captain	Royal Army Medical Corps	Invalided, May 1915	Mentioned in Despatches twice	France, 1914
DAVIDSON, William Stanley	Private	Captain	16th Battn. The Manchester Regiment	Wounded, July 1916	—	France, 1915-1916.
DAVIE, Thomas	2nd Lieutenant	2nd Lieutenant	The Cameronians (Scottish Rifles)	—	—	—
DAVIS, Alexander McLachlan	Private	Private	Canadian Expeditionary Force	Wounded, November 1915	—	France
DAVIS, Alfred George	Private	Lieutenant	8th Battn. Argyll & Sutherland Highlanders	—	Military Cross	France, 1917-1918
DEACON, Colin	2nd Lieutenant	2nd Lieutenant	Royal Engineers	—	—	—
DICK, Arnold J.	Captain	Captain	5th Battn. Highland Light Infantry	Wounded, August 1917	—	France, 1916-1917
✠ DICK, Watson Tulloch	Private	Captain	9th (G.H.) Battn. Highland Light Infantry. The 7th Battn. The South Wales Borderers	Killed in action, 18th September, 1918, at Grand Cousonne	Military Cross	France, 1915-1917 Salonica, 1917-1918
✠ DICKSON, Hugh Barclay	2nd Lieutenant	Captain	The Black Watch (Royal Highlanders)	Wounded, July 1916 Killed in action, 12th October, 1917, at Passchendale	—	France, 1916-1917

Name.	Rank. At beginning of War or on joining.	Rank. At end of War.	Unit.	Casualties.	Honours or Decorations.	Field of Service.
DICKSON, James Douglas Hamilton	Private	Private	Canadian Forces	—	—	—
DICKSON, John Harold	Midshipman	Sub-Lieutenant	Royal Navy	—	—	At Sea
DISHINGTON, Isaac	2nd Lieutenant	2nd Lieutenant	Royal Garrison Artillery	—	—	Home Service
✠ DISHINGTON, William	Private	Sergeant	Royal Army Veterinary Corps	Died of wounds, 26th October, 1918	—	France, 1916–1918
DIXON, Arthur	Private	Lieutenant	Royal Engineers	—	—	France, 1917–1918
DIXON, James Ferrie	2nd Lieutenant	2nd Lieutenant	Argyll & Sutherland Highlanders	Wounded	—	—
DIXON, John George	Private	Private	28th London Regiment (Artists' Rifles)	—	—	—
✠ DOBSON, Edward	Private	Captain	17th Battn. Highland Light Infantry	Wounded, November 1916 Killed in action, 10th July, 1917, at Nieuport	—	France, 1916–1917
DOBSON, John	2nd Lieutenant	Captain	5th Battn. The Cameronians (Scottish Rifles) 17th Battn. King's Royal Rifle Corps	Wounded, April 1918	Military Cross	France and Flanders, 1917–1918
DOBSON, William Sharpe	3rd Air Mechanic	2nd Air Craftsman	Royal Flying Corps	—	—	France, 1918

NAME.	RANK. At beginning of War or on joining.	RANK. At end of War.	UNIT.	CASUALTIES.	HONOURS OR DECORATIONS.	FIELD OF SERVICE.
DODDS, William E.	Cadet	2nd Lieutenant	Glasgow University Officers Training Corps Kings Own Yorkshire Light Infantry	—	—	—
DONALD, Andrew Patrick	Corporal	Corporal	Royal Army Service Corps	Wounded	—	—
DONALD, Graham	Flight Sub-Lieutenant	Major	Royal Naval Air Service Royal Air Force	—	Mentioned in Despatches Distinguished Flying Cross Hellenic War Cross	North Sea, 1915–1917 Dardanelles, Struma, Doiran, Constantinople, Aegean, 1917–1918
DONALD, Ronald J.	Trooper	Trooper	Lothians & Border Horse	—	—	—
DONALD, Thomas Colin	Cadet	Cadet	Glasgow University Officers Training Corps	—	—	Home Service
DONALDSON, George	Cadet	Cadet	Glasgow University Officers Training Corps	—	—	Home Service
DONALDSON, J. W.	Lieutenant	Captain	Royal Army Service Corps	—	—	—
DOW, Eric	Cadet	Cadet	Glasgow University Officers Training Corps	—	—	Home Service
✠ DOWNIE, James Maitland	Lieutenant	Captain	Royal Army Medical Corps	Died, 26th October, 1918, at Basra	—	Mesopotamia, 1916–1918

Name.	Rank. At beginning of War or on joining.	At end of War.	Unit.	Casualties.	Honours or Decorations.	Field of Service.
✠ DOWNIE, Robert Theodore Manners	2nd Lieutenant	Lieutenant	5th Battn. Highland Light Infantry	Died, 24th January, 1916	—	Home Service
DRON, Alan Wilson	Sapper	Sapper	Royal Engineers	—	—	Home Service
✠ DRON, John Kent	Private	Lieutenant	9th (G.H.) Battn. Highland Light Infantry 6th Battn. Highland Light Infantry	Killed in action, 13th October, 1918	—	France, 1914-1915 and 1918
DRON, Robert L. A.	Sapper	Lieutenant	Royal Engineers	Invalided, August 1916 Wounded, April 1918	—	France, 1915-1916, 1918
DRON, William	Company Sergeant-Major	Captain	9th (G.H.) Battn. Highland Light Infantry 21st Battn. Highland Light Infantry	—	—	France, 1918
✠ DUCKETT, Harold Ager	Private	2nd Lieutenant	Royal Engineers 9th (G.H.) Battn. Highland Light Infantry	Died of wounds, 7th June, 1917	—	France, 1914-1917
✠ DUCKETT, Kenneth Lees	Private	2nd Lieutenant	9th (G.H.) Battn. Highland Light Infantry	Wounded, May 1915 Died of wounds, 22nd August, 1916	—	France, 1914-1916
DUFFUS, Percy B.	2nd Lieutenant	Captain	The Black Watch (Royal Highlanders)	—	—	—

NAME.	RANK. At beginning of War or on joining.	RANK. At end of War.	UNIT.	CASUALTIES.	HONOURS OR DECORATIONS.	FIELD OF SERVICE.
DUN, Thomas Ingram	Captain	Major	Royal Army Medical Corps	Wounded, October 1916	Mentioned in Despatches three times Military Cross Distinguished Service Order	France, 1915–1918
DUNBAR, Lyon Wilson	Cadet	Cadet	Glasgow University Officers Training Corps	—	—	Home Service
DUNCAN, Charles W. L.	Cadet	2nd Lieutenant	Edinburgh University Officers Training Corps Royal Horse Artillery	—	—	—
✠ DUNCAN, Robert	Sub-Lieutenant	Lieutenant	'Anson' Battn. Royal Naval Division	Killed in action, 8th May, 1915, at Cape Helles	—	Antwerp Expedition, 1914 Dardanelles, 1915
DUNCAN, Robert H. L.	Corporal	Corporal	9th (G.H.) Battn. Highland Light Infantry	—	—	France and Belgium, 1914–1918
DUNCANSON, James Gray	2nd Lieutenant	Major	Royal Army Medical Corps	—	Mentioned in Despatches twice	France, 1917–1918
DUNCANSON, John	Captain	Captain	Canadian Expeditionary Force	Wounded, September 1916	—	France, 1915–1916
DUNCANSON, R. Kenneth	2nd Lieutenant	Lieutenant	6th Battn. Highland Light Infantry	Wounded, September 1916 Wounded, November 1916	—	France, 1916 East Africa, 1918
DUNCANSON, Thomas H.	2nd Lieutenant	Lieutenant	7th Battn. Highland Light Infantry	Invalided, August 1917 Invalided, December 1917	—	British German and Portuguese East Africa, 1916-1918

Name.	Rank. At beginning of War or on joining.	Rank. At end of War.	Unit.	Casualties.	Honours or Decorations.	Field of Service.
DUNLOP, Andrew, Junior	Lieutenant	Lieutenant	7th Batn. The Cameronians (Scottish Rifles)	Wounded, 1917 twice	—	Egypt and Palestine, 1916–1918; France, 1918
DUNLOP, Douglas H.	2nd Lieutenant	Captain	Royal Engineers	Wounded, July 1916	Mentioned in Despatches; Military Cross	France and Belgium, 1915–1918
DUNLOP, Herbert R.	Lieutenant	Lieutenant	Royal Field Artillery	—	Military Cross	—
DUNN, Bannatyne	Lieutenant	Lieut.-Commander	Royal Naval Volunteer Reserve	—	—	Home Service
DUNN, Fred	Lieutenant	Captain	Royal Naval Volunteer Reserve	Wounded, August 1918	Military Cross	Dardanelles, 1915–1916; France, 1917–1918
✠ DUNN, Herbert	Private	2nd Lieutenant	The Royal Fusiliers; 8th Batn. The Cameronians (Scottish Rifles)	Died, 25th October, 1915, at Alexandria	—	Gallipoli, 1915
DUNN, James Churchill	Captain	Captain	Royal Army Medical Corps	Gassed, May 1918; Wounded, September 1918	Mentioned in Despatches; Military Cross; Bar to Military Cross; Distinguished Service Order	France and Belgium, 1915–1918
✠ DUNN, John	2nd Lieutenant	2nd Lieutenant	The Cameronians (Scottish Rifles)	Killed in action, 21st June, 1917	—	France

Name.	Rank. At beginning of War or on joining.	Rank. At end of War.	Unit.	Casualties.	Honours or Decorations.	Field of Service.
DUNN, William A.	2nd Lieutenant	Captain	Argyll & Sutherland Highlanders	Wounded, December 1915 and November 1916	Mentioned in Despatches	France, 1915-1917
DUNN, Willoughby Middleton	2nd Lieutenant	Lieutenant	8th Battn. Highland Light Infantry	—	—	Home Service
EADIE, Eric Macgregor	Wireless Officer	Sub-Lieutenant	Royal Navy Royal Naval Air Service	Torpedoed	—	At Sea, 1917-1918
EADIE, Norman	Private	2nd Lieutenant	9th (G.H.) Battn. Highland Light Infantry	Wounded, June 1916	—	France
EASTON, Alexander L.	Private	Private	Burma Railway Volunteers	—	—	Burma
✚ EASTON, Arthur Aitken	2nd Lieutenant	2nd Lieutenant	10th Battn. Highland Light Infantry	Killed in action, 2nd March, 1916	Mentioned in Despatches	France, 1915-1916
EASTON, Arthur Charles	Flight Cadet	Flight Cadet	Royal Air Force	—	—	Home Service
✚ EASTON, Thomas Henderson	Lieutenant	Lieutenant	Royal Naval Volunteer Reserve	Died on service, 21st August, 1916	—	Home Service
EDWARD, D. Herbert	Private	2nd Lieutenant	Highland Light Infantry	—	—	—
ELDRED, Charles Harold	Corporal	2nd Lieutenant	Highland Light Infantry Argyll & Sutherland Highlanders	—	—	—

Name.	Rank. At beginning of War or on joining.	Rank. At end of War.	Unit.	Casualties.	Honours or Decorations.	Field of Service.
✠ ELDER, Charles Moncrieff	Private	Private	9th (G.H.) Battn. Highland Light Infantry	Killed in action, 26th September, 1917	—	France, 1916–1917
✠ ELLIOT, Alexander Shiels	2nd Lieutenant	Lieutenant	8th Battn. Highland Light Infantry	Killed in action, 28th June, 1915, at Cape Helles	—	Gallipoli, 1915
ELLIOT, Walter Elliot	Lieutenant	Captain	Royal Army Medical Corps	Wounded, October 1918	Military Cross / Bar to Military Cross	France and Belgium, 1914–1918
ELLIS, Clement	Cadet	Cadet	Glasgow University Officers Training Corps / 9th Officer Cadet Battalion	—	—	Home Service
ELLIS, Thomas	Lieutenant	Lieutenant	Argyll & Sutherland Highlanders	—	—	—
ERSKINE, J. A. Dixon	Captain	Captain	9th Battn. Argyll & Sutherland Highlanders	Invalided, 1916	—	Home Service
ERSKINE, Thomas Marshall	Air Mechanic	Air Mechanic	Royal Air Force	—	—	Home Service
✠ FAWCETT, Cyril John	Private	Private	17th Battn. Highland Light Infantry	Killed in action, 1st July, 1916	—	France, 1915–1916
FERGUS, Andrew	Gunner	Gunner	Edinburgh University Officers Training Corps	—	—	Home Service
FERGUS, Andrew Macfadyen Houston	2nd Lieutenant	2nd Lieutenant	8th Battn. Seaforth Highlanders	Invalided, January 1915	—	Home Service

NAME.	RANK. At beginning of War or on joining.	RANK. At end of War.	UNIT.	CASUALTIES.	HONOURS OR DECORATIONS.	FIELD OF SERVICE.
FERGUSSON, Archibald Napier	Private	Lieutenant	9th (G.H.) Battn. Highland Light Infantry	Invalided, January 1917	—	France, 1914-1916, 1917 and 1918
FERGUSON, Hugh	Cadet	Lieutenant	8th Battn. Argyll & Sutherland Highlanders	—	—	France, 1918
✠ FERGUSON, Thomas Jenkins	2nd Lieutenant	2nd Lieutenant	Royal Tank Corps	Killed in action, 30th August, 1918	—	France
FERGUSON, William	Private	Lieutenant	9th (G.H.) Battn. Highland Light Infantry 15th Battn. Highland Light Infantry	Invalided, May 1916	Military Cross French War Cross	France, 1915-1918
FERGUSON, William Grierson	Cadet	Gunner	Edinburgh University Officers Training Corps	—	—	Home Service
FERRIER, George Stratton	Private	2nd Lieutenant	Labour Corps	—	—	Home Service
FINDLAY, Ian Crawford	Private	Lieutenant	Scottish Horse Royal Field Artillery	Wounded	Mentioned in Despatches Military Cross Bar to Military Cross Order of St. Anne	France, 1916-1918
✠ FINDLAY, Matthew	Private	Lance-Corporal	New Zealand Expeditionary Forces	Wounded, September 1915 Died of wounds, 29th May, 1916	—	Egypt, 1914-1915 Gallipoli, 1915

NAME.	RANK.		UNIT.	CASUALTIES.	HONOURS OR DECORATIONS.	FIELD OF SERVICE.
	At beginning of War or on joining.	At end of War.				
FINDLAY, Robert	Gunner	Gunner	Edinburgh University Officers Training Corps	—	—	Home Service
✠ FINDLAY, Struthers	Private	2nd Lieutenant	5th Battn. The Queen's Own Cameron Highlanders Lowland Cyclist Company	Wounded, August 1915. Killed in action, 4th August, 1916, at Romani	—	France, 1914–1915. Egypt, 1916
✠ FINDLAY, Walter	Private	Lance-Corporal	9th Battn. The Royal Sussex Regiment	Reported missing, September 1915, at Loos	—	France, 1915
FINDLAY, William Robert	Private	Lieutenant	The Buffs (East Kent Regiment)	Wounded, August 1918	—	France, 1918
FINLAY, Randal G.	Lieutenant	Lieutenant	Royal Field Artillery	—	—	Suvla, 1915
FINLAY, William George Knox	2nd Lieutenant	Captain	Royal Field Artillery	Invalided	—	Home Service
FISHER, Joseph Edgely	Cadet	2nd Lieutenant	Glasgow University Officers Training Corps King's Own Royal Lancashire Regiment	Wounded and prisoner. Repatriated	—	—
FLEMING, William	Cadet	Cadet	Glasgow University Officers Training Corps Royal Air Force	—	—	—
FORBES, James	2nd Lieutenant	2nd Lieutenant	Argyll & Sutherland Highlanders	Wounded, December 1916	—	France, June 1916–1918

NAME.	RANK. At beginning of War or on joining.	RANK. At end of War.	UNIT.	CASUALTIES.	HONOURS OR DECORATIONS.	FIELD OF SERVICE.
FORRESTER, Alexander Roxburgh	Cadet	2nd Lieutenant	Royal Garrison Artillery	—	—	Home Service
FORRESTER, John Francis M.	Private	Private	Highland Light Infantry	—	—	—
FORRESTER, William Roxburgh	Private	Lieutenant	15th Battn, The Royal Scots (Royal Regiment) 11th Battn. Gordon Highlanders Royal Field Artillery	—	Military Cross	France, 1915 Mesopotamia, 1916–1918 Persia, 1918
FORSYTH, M. Halford	Private	Private	Labour Battalion	—	—	—
FORSYTH, Walter William	Private	2nd Lieutenant	Training Reserve Battn. Highland Light Infantry	—	—	—
FOTHERINGHAM, David	Private	Private	Scottish Horse	Invalided November 1917	—	Gallipoli
FOTHERINGHAM, Eric	Trooper	2nd Lieutenant	Scottish Horse Royal Field Artillery	Wounded	—	—
FOTHERINGHAM, James Bryan	Lieutenant	Captain	Royal Army Medical Corps	Invalided, 1917	Mentioned in Despatches	France, 1915 Mediterranean, 1915–1916 Egypt, 1916–1917 East Africa, 1917 Italy, 1918

Name.	Rank. At beginning of War or on joining.	Rank. At end of War.	Unit.	Casualties.	Honours or Decorations.	Field of Service
FOTHERINGHAM, William	Lieutenant	Captain	Royal Army Medical Corps	Gassed, 1918	Mentioned in Despatches twice; Military Cross; Bar to Military Cross	France, 1914–1918
✠ FOULIS, James Bell	Private	Captain	5th Battn. Queen's Own Cameron Highlanders	Wounded, February 1915; Killed in action, 18th October, 1916	—	France, 1915–1916
FRAME, A. Car	Lieutenant	Captain	9th (G.H.) Battn. Highland Light Infantry	Wounded, December 1914; Wounded, July 1916	Mentioned in Despatches; Distinguished Service Order	France, 1914–1917
✠ FRASER, Alistair Ian Stuart	Private	Private	6th Battn. Queen's Own Cameron Highlanders	Killed in action, September 1915, at Loos	—	France, 1915
FRASER, Archibald	Transport Driver	Transport Driver	British Red Cross Transport	—	—	Home Service
FRASER, Donald	Lieutenant	Lieutenant	28th London Regiment (Artists Rifles). The Essex Regiment	—	—	Home Service
FRASER, James Spiers	Private	Private	The Cameronians (Scottish Rifles)	—	—	—
FRASER, James Wright	Private	Lieutenant	17th Battn. Highland Light Infantry 10th Corps Cyclist Battn.	Invalided, November 1918	—	Belgium and France, 1915–1918

Name.	Rank. At beginning of War or on joining.	Rank. At end of War.	Unit.	Casualties.	Honours or Decorations.	Field of Service.
FRASER, John	Cadet	Bombardier	Edinburgh University Officers Training Corps	—	—	Home Service
FRASER, Thomas	Sergeant	Sergeant	Medical Dept. United States Army	—	—	Home Service in America
FRASER, William C.	Private	Lieutenant	28th Punjabis (Indian Army)	—	—	India
FREW, Alexander	Private	Captain	9th (G.H.) Battn. Highland Light Infantry	—	Mentioned in Despatches	France, 1914-1918
FREW, George	Private	Private	9th (G.H.) Battn. Highland Light Infantry	Wounded, February 1915	—	France, 1914-1915
FREW, Gordon Thomson	2nd Lieutenant	Lieutenant	Labour Corps	—	—	France, 1917-1918
FREW, Robert	Cadet	Lieutenant	Royal Artillery	Wounded, October 1918	—	France, 1918
FREW, R. L. Hector	Lieutenant	Lieutenant	9th (G.H.) Battn. Highland Light Infantry	Wounded, April 1918	—	France, 1918
FULTON, Cecil S.	2nd Lieutenant	Captain	Royal Scots Fusiliers Royal Flying Corps Royal Air Force	—	—	—
FULTON, John Muirhead	Lance-Corporal	Lance-Corporal	Highland Cyclist Battn.	—	—	—
FULTON, Walter	Gunner	Gunner	Royal Garrison Artillery	—	—	—

NAME.	RANK. At beginning of War or on joining.	RANK. At end of War.	UNIT.	CASUALTIES.	HONOURS OR DECORATIONS.	FIELD OF SERVICE.
FULTON, William W. E.	Cadet	2nd Lieutenant	Glasgow University Officers Training Corps Royal Scots Fusiliers	—	—	—
FYFE, Ronald Watson	Midshipman	Midshipman	Royal Navy	—	—	Gallipoli, 1915
✠ GALBRAITH, David Boyd	2nd Lieutenant	2nd Lieutenant	7th Battn. Highland Light Infantry	Wounded, 12th July, 1915 Killed in action, 20th August, 1915, at Dardanelles	—	—
GALBRAITH, James Alexander	Cadet	2nd Lieutenant	Royal Flying Corps Cadet Battn. Royal Air Force	—	—	—
GALBRAITH, James Hardie	Lieut.-Colonel	Lieut.-Colonel	7th Battn. Highland Light Infantry	Invalided, December 1915 Invalided, December 1917	Mentioned in Despatches Order of St. Maurice and St. Lazarus 4th Class	Gallipoli, 1915 Egypt and Palestine, 1916-1917
✠ GALBRAITH, Norman Dunlop	Trooper	Lieutenant	Queen's Own Royal Glasgow Yeomanry 7th Battn. Highland Light Infantry	Killed, 22nd August, 1918	—	Gallipoli, 1915 Egypt, 1916-1917 France, 1917-1918
GALBRAITH, Robert Jack	Private	Lieutenant	Royal Garrison Artillery	Gassed, September 1918 and Invalided	—	France, 1917-1918
GALBRAITH, Thomas Dunlop	Lieutenant	Lieutenant-Commander	Royal Navy	—	—	Grand Fleet, 1914 Dardanelles, 1915 Grand Fleet, 1915-1918

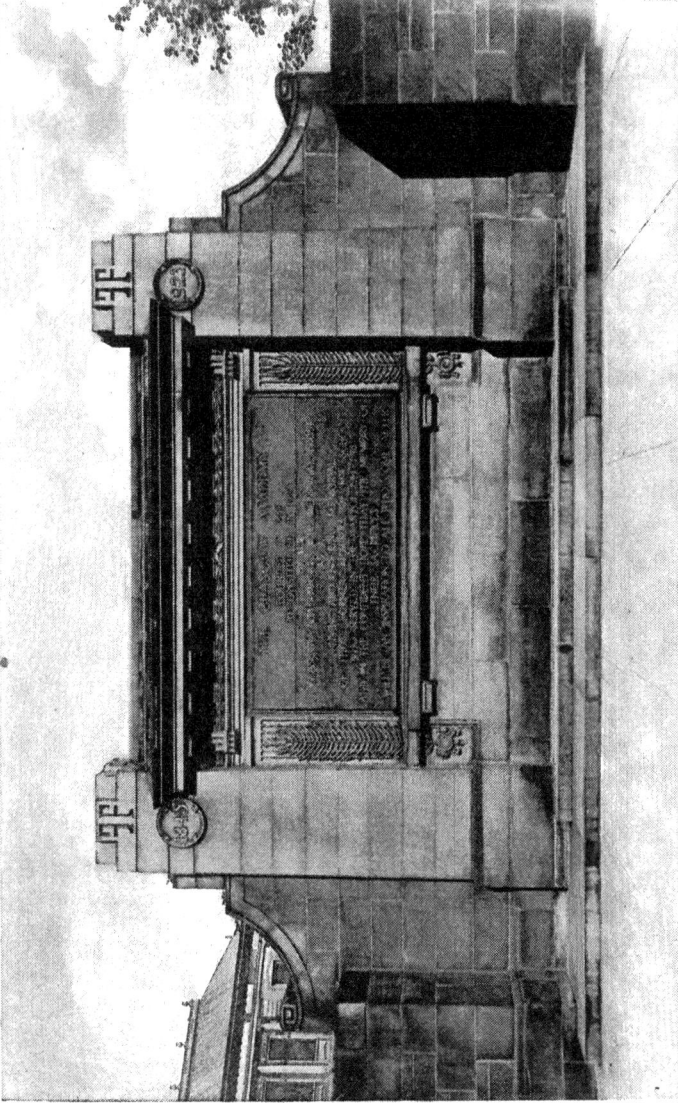

THE WAR MEMORIAL

NAME.	RANK. At beginning of War or on joining.	RANK. At end of War.	UNIT.	CASUALTIES.	HONOURS OR DECORATIONS.	FIELD OF SERVICE.
GALBRAITH, Walter Weir	2nd Lieutenant	Captain	Royal Army Medical Corps	—	—	France, 1915–1917 Italy, 1917–1918
✠ GALBRAITH, William Brodie	Lieutenant	Lieutenant	7th Battn. Highland Light Infantry	Died of wounds on 14th July, 1915	—	Gallipoli, 1915
GALLIE, Arthur Holmes	Lieutenant	Lieutenant	Queen's Own Royal Glasgow Yeomanry	Prisoner of War, 1918	—	France, 1917–1918
GALLIE, Robert Arthur	2nd Lieutenant	Captain	Queen's Own Royal Glasgow Yeomanry	—	Mentioned in Despatches six times Military Cross Belgian War Cross	France, 1915–1918
✠ GARDNER, John	2nd Lieutenant	Captain	7th Battn. Royal Scots Fusiliers	Wounded, September 1915 Wounded, May 1916 Wounded, 22nd August, 1917 and died, 27th September, 1917	Mentioned in Despatches Military Cross	France, 1915–1917
GARDNER, Matthew	Private	Major	17th Battn. Highland Light Infantry	—	—	France and Salonica
GARDNER, William B.	Private	Captain	Queen's Own Cameron Highlanders The Royal Scots (Royal Regiment)	Wounded, September 1915	—	France, 1915–1917

D

Name.	Rank. At beginning of War or on joining.	Rank. At end of War.	Unit.	Casualties.	Honours or Decorations.	Field of Service.
GEMMELL, Norman L.	Sergeant	Sergeant	17th Battn. Highland Light Infantry	Invalided, July 1916–December 1916. Prisoner of War, August 1918–December 1918	Military Medal	France and Belgium, 1915–1918
GEMMELL, Ralph L.	Private	Private	14th Battn. Highland Light Infantry	Prisoner of War, April 1918–December 1918	—	France, 1917–1918
GEMMELL, Robert	Cadet	Cadet	Edinburgh University Officers Training Corps	—	—	Home Service
✠ GEMMELL, Stewart Armour	Captain	Captain	6th Battn. Highland Light Infantry	Wounded on 12th July, 1915, and died, 22nd July, 1915	—	Gallipoli, 1915
GEMMILL, Alexander	Private	Lieutenant	3rd Battn. The Cameronians (Scottish Rifles)	—	—	India, 1916. Mesopotamia, 1918
✠ GEMMILL, John Adshead	2nd Lieutenant	2nd Lieutenant	16th Battn. Highland Light Infantry	Wounded, February 1916. Killed in action, 1st July, 1916	—	France 1915–1916
GEMMILL, William C.	Gunner	Bombardier	Royal Field Artillery	—	—	—
GENTLES, Matthew Page	Corporal	Corporal	The Cameronians (Scottish Rifles)	Invalided	—	—
✠ GENTLES, Thomas	—	Sergeant	5th Battn. The Cameronians (Scottish Rifles)	Died on Service, 3rd January, 1917	—	Home Service

NAME.	RANK. At beginning of War or on joining.	RANK. At end of War.	UNIT.	CASUALTIES.	HONOURS OR DECORATIONS.	FIELD OF SERVICE.
✠ GENTLES, William R.	Private	Sergeant	5th Battn. The Cameronians (Scottish Rifles)	Died on Service, 18th July, 1918	—	—
GERSON, Samuel	Private	Private	Royal Army Medical Corps	—	—	—
GERSTENBERG, Eric G.	Cadet	Cadet	Glasgow University Officers Training Corps	—	—	Home Service
GERSTENBERG, Ralph Alexander	Private	Lieutenant	Argyll & Sutherland Highlanders	Wounded, May 1918 Prisoner of War, 1918	—	France, 1918
GERSTENBERG, Vivian	Cadet	Cadet	Glasgow University Officers Training Corps	—	—	Home Service
✠ GIBSON, James Douglas	2nd Lieutenant	Lieutenant	Royal Engineers	Killed in action, 25th March, 1918	—	France
GILCHRIST, Hector Gordon	Lieutenant	Lieut.-Colonel	Royal Engineers Royal Corps of Signals	—	Mentioned in Despatches four times Military Cross Distinguished Service Order	France, 1914–1918
GILFILLAN, William Wallace	Private	Lieutenant	Inns of Court Officers Training Corps 9th (G.H.) Battn. Highland Light Infantry	Wounded, June 1917	—	France, 1917
GILLESPIE, W. Scott	Private	Private	Highland Light Infantry Lowland Division Cyclist Corps	Wounded	—	—

Name.	Rank. At beginning of War or on joining.	Rank. At end of War.	Unit.	Casualties.	Honours or Decorations.	Field of Service.
GILLIES, W. Don	2nd Lieutenant	2nd Lieutenant	Argyll & Sutherland Highlanders	Wounded	—	—
✠ GILMOUR, James	2nd Lieutenant	2nd Lieutenant	The Cameronians (Scottish Rifles)	Killed in action, 30th March, 1918	—	France
GLEN, Archibald	Private	Lance-Corporal	11th Battn. Duke of Cambridge's Own (Middlesex Regiment)	Prisoner of War, 1917	—	France, 1917
GLEN, A. Ernest	Lieutenant	Lieutenant	8th Battn. The Cameronians (Scottish Rifles)	Wounded, November 1917	—	France, 1917
GLEN, John Frew	Private	Sergeant	New Zealand Infantry	Wounded, 1916 Invalided, 1917	Distinguished Conduct Medal	Gallipoli and France
GOODALL, Frederick Galt	Private	Lieutenant	9th (G.H.) Battn. Highland Light Infantry 6th Scottish Rifles	Wounded	Military Cross	France, 1914–1918
GORDON, Evan R. M.	Lieutenant	Lieutenant	88th Carnatic Infantry (Indian Army)	—	—	India
GORDON, John Miller	Surgeon	Surgeon-Commander	Royal Navy	—	—	East Indies Station (India, Ceylon, East Africa, Red Sea and Suez Canal)
✠ GORDON, Robert Hope	2nd Lieutenant	2nd Lieutenant	8th Battn. The King's Liverpool Regiment	Wounded, July 1915 Missing, August 1916	—	France, 1915–1916

NAME.	RANK. At beginning of War or on joining.	RANK. At end of War.	UNIT.	CASUALTIES.	HONOURS OR DECORATIONS.	FIELD OF SERVICE.
✠ GORDON-SMITH, Gordon	2nd Lieutenant	Captain	Royal West Kent Regiment	Killed in action, 24th October, 1918	—	France
✠ GORDON-SMITH, Norman	2nd Lieutenant	2nd Lieutenant	Highland Light Infantry Royal Flying Corps	Killed in action, 19th December, 1915	—	France
GRAHAM, Alexander Gillespie	Captain	Lieut.-Colonel	6th Battn. The Cameronians (Scottish Rifles) 6th Battn. Seaforth Highlanders	Wounded, January 1917 Invalided, December 1918	Mentioned in Despatches Military Cross	France, 1915–1917
✠ GRAHAM, Archibald Stuart Bulloch	Lieutenant	Lieutenant	Gordon Highlanders	Killed in action, 31st October, 1914, at Ypres	Mentioned in Despatches	France, 1914
GRAHAM, Douglas A. H.	Lieutenant	Captain	The Cameronians (Scottish Rifles)	Wounded, October 1914	Mentioned in Despatches Military Cross French War Cross	France and Belgium, 1916–1918
✠ GRAHAM, George Wilson	2nd Lieutenant	2nd Lieutenant	Royal Air Force	Killed in action, 13th July, 1918	—	Belgium, 1918
GRAHAM, J. Murray	2nd Lieutenant	Lieutenant	Army Ordnance Department	Invalided	Mentioned in Despatches	Salonica, 1916–1918
GRAHAM, J. R. B.	Private	Lieutenant	Canadian Army Pay Corps	—	—	—
GRAHAM, James Gibson	Lieutenant	Lieutenant	Royal Field Artillery	Invalided, August 1918	—	France and Belgium, 1917–1918
GRAHAM, John Gibson	2nd Lieutenant	Captain	Royal Scots Fusiliers	—	Military Cross	—

NAME.	RANK. At beginning of War or on joining.	RANK. At end of War.	UNIT.	CASUALTIES.	HONOURS OR DECORATIONS.	FIELD OF SERVICE.
GRAHAM, John P.	Captain	Captain	Egyptian Labour Corps	—	—	—
GRAHAM, Mungo Alan	Private	Captain	Rhodesia Regiment South African Infantry	Invalided, 1917 Prisoner of War, 1918	—	East Africa, 1915–1917 France, 1918
GRAHAM, Patrick H.	Private	Captain	17th Battn. Highland Light Infantry	Wounded, April 1918	—	France, 1916–1918
GRAHAM-BROWN, Colin	Bombardier	Corporal	Singapore Volunteer Artillery	—	—	—
GRAHAM-BROWN, Edward D.	2nd Lieutenant	Lieutenant	Royal Field Artillery	Invalided twice	—	France, 1915 Mesopotamia, 1915–1916 India, 1916–1917 Palestine, 1917–1918
GRAHAM-BROWN, George Francis	2nd Lieutenant	Captain	6th Battn. King's Own Scottish Borderers	Wounded, May 1916 Invalided, September 1918	—	France, 1916
✠ GRANT, Charles Bruce	2nd Lieutenant	Lieutenant	9th (G.H.) Battn. Highland Light Infantry	Died of wounds, 6th December, 1917	—	France
GRANT, James Warwick	Private	Captain	9th (G.H.) Battn. Highland Light Infantry 5th Battn. Queen's Own Cameron Highlanders King's African Rifles	Wounded, July 1916	Military Cross	France, 1915–1916 German East Africa, 1917–1918

NAME.	RANK. At beginning of War or on joining.	RANK. At end of War.	UNIT.	CASUALTIES.	HONOURS OR DECORATIONS.	FIELD OF SERVICE.
GRANT, Norman Carlos	2nd Lieutenant	Captain	6th Battn. King's Own Scottish Borderers	—	Military Cross	France, 1915–1918
GRANT, Pharic	Major	Colonel	Royal Field Artillery	Invalided, 1917–1918	—	Egypt, 1916–1918
GRANT, Theodore Douglas	Private	Lieutenant	4th Battn. The Cameronians (Scottish Rifles)	Wounded, August 1918	—	Mesopotamia, Persia and Caucasus, 1916–1918
GRAY, A. Arthur	Private	Private	Royal Field Artillery	—	—	Home Service
GRAY, Alexander Mungo	Captain	Major	5th Battn. The Cameronians (Scottish Rifles)	Invalided, May 1915–May 1916	Mentioned in Despatches twice Officer of the Order of the British Empire	France, 1914–1918
GRAY, David D.	2nd Lieutenant	Major	Royal Garrison Artillery	Wounded, September 1918	Mentioned in Despatches twice Order of the Crown of Belgium 5th Class Belgian War Cross	France, 1916–1918
GRAY, Donald	Lieutenant	Lieutenant	Royal Navy	—	—	Mediterranean, 1917–1918
GRAY, J. Lindsay	Cadet	Cadet	Edinburgh University Officers Training Corps	—	—	Home Service
GRAY, James Wilson Sholto	Corporal	2nd Lieutenant	Royal Flying Corps The Cameronians (Scottish Rifles)	—	—	—

NAME.	RANK. At beginning of War or on joining.	RANK. At end of War.	UNIT.	CASUALTIES.	HONOURS OR DECORATIONS.	FIELD OF SERVICE.
✠ GRAY, John	Lieutenant	Lieutenant	8th Battn. Argyll & Sutherland Highlanders	Killed in action, October 1918, at Villiers Guislain	—	France, 1918
GRAY, Joseph Russell	Private	Lieutenant	Royal Army Service Corps	Invalided, May 1917	—	Home Service
✠ GRAY, Magnus N.	2nd Lieutenant	Lieutenant	The Cameronians (Scottish Rifles)	Killed in action, 21st June, 1915	Mentioned in Despatches	France
GRAY, Oliver	Driver	Sub-Lieutenant	British Red Cross Royal Navy	—	—	Italy, 1916 At Sea, 1917–1918
GRAY, William L.	Colonel	Colonel	Royal Army Medical Corps	—	—	—
GREENLEES, William	Cadet	2nd Lieutenant	The Royal Scots (Royal Regiment)	—	—	Home Service
GREGORY, Alexander	Gunner	Cadet	Royal Field Artillery Officer Cadet Battn.	—	—	—
GREGORY, Andrew Duncan	Cadet	2nd Lieutenant	Royal Scots Fusiliers	—	—	Home Service
GREGORY, Christopher John	Cadet	Cadet	Glasgow University Officers Training Corps	—	—	Home Service
GREGORY, James Lochhead	Captain	Surgeon-Lieutenant	Royal Army Medical Corps Royal Navy	Invalided, December 1915	—	Mediterranean, 1915 France, 1916–1918 Royal Navy, Dover Patrol, 1918

NAME.	RANK. At beginning of War on joining.	RANK. At end of War.	UNIT.	CASUALTIES.	HONOURS OR DECORATIONS.	FIELD OF SERVICE.
GREGORY, John Bonar	Private	Lieutenant	7th Battn. Argyll & Sutherland Highlanders	—	—	France, 1916–1918
GREGORY, William Stothert	Corporal	Corporal	17th Battn. Highland Light Infantry	Wounded, July 1916	—	France, 1915–1916
GREIG, Arthur Gordon	2nd Lieutenant	Captain	Gordon Highlanders	Wounded, September 1915 Invalided, January 1918	—	France, 1915
GREIG, D. Herbert	Private	Private	Canadian Expeditionary Force	—	—	—
GREIG, Douglas Stewart	Private	Captain	9th (G.H.) Battn. Highland Light Infantry The Black Watch (Royal Highlanders)	Prisoner of War, 1918	Military Cross	France, 1916–1918
GREIG, John Young Thomson	Corporal	Captain	Royal Army Medical Corps The Northumberland Fusiliers	—	—	France, 1918
GREIG, Kenneth B. S.	Paymaster-Lieutenant	Paymaster-Lieutenant	Royal Navy Royal Naval Air Service Royal Air Force	—	Mentioned in Despatches	China Station, 1914–1915 Grand Fleet, 1915–1917 Adriatic, Anti-Submarine Patrol, February 1918 Aegean, Mine Sweeping, September 1918

Name.	Rank. At beginning of War or on joining.	Rank. At end of War.	Unit.	Casualties.	Honours or Decorations.	Field of Service.
GREIG, Louis L.	Surgeon-Commander	Wing-Commander	Royal Navy / Royal Air Force	Prisoner of War, Germany, 1914-1915	Legion of Honour / Croix de Guerre / Medaille Militaire	France and Belgium, 1914 / France, 1917
GREIG, Patrick	Captain	Major	6th Battn. Highland Light Infantry	—	—	—
GRIERSON, Alexander Faill	2nd Lieutenant	Captain	5th Battn. The Cameronians (Scottish Rifles)	Wounded	Military Cross / French War Cross	France, 1914-1918
✠ GRIERSON, Lieutenant General Sir James Moncrieff, K.C.B., C.M.G., C.V.O.	Lieutenant-General	Lieutenant-General	Staff	Died on Service, 17th August, 1914	—	France, 1914
GRIERSON, John Murray	2nd Lieutenant	Major	5th Battn. The Cameronians (Scottish Rifles)	Wounded, November 1916	Mentioned in Despatches twice	France, 1914-1916 / East Africa, 1917-1918
✠ GRIEVE, William Robertson	Lieutenant	Lieutenant	7th Battn. Highland Light Infantry	Killed in action, April 1917	—	France, 1917
GRIGG, Stanley James	Private	Private	Highland Light Infantry	—	—	—
GRISCHOTTI, William	Lieutenant	Captain	The King's Shropshire Light Infantry	Wounded	—	—
GUNN, George Gibson	Private	Regimental Quarter-master-Sergeant	Canadian Expeditionary Force	—	—	France and Belgium, 1916-1918

Name.	Rank. At beginning of War or on joining.	Rank. At end of War.	Unit.	Casualties.	Honours or Decorations.	Field of Service.
GUNN, John Leith	Lieutenant	Captain	Canadian Expeditionary Force Pay Corps	—	—	Canada
✠ GUTHRIE, Charles Wilfrid	2nd Lieutenant	2nd Lieutenant	The Royal Scots (Royal Regiment)	Killed in action, August 1917	—	France, 1917
GUTHRIE, Lester	Despatch Rider	Corporal	Royal Engineers	—	—	—
GUTHRIE, Robert Neil	Captain	Lieut.-Colonel	New Zealand Medical Corps	Wounded, May 1915, 9th August, 1915, and 21st August, 1915	Mentioned in Despatches Military Cross	Egypt, 1914 Gallipoli, 1915 France, 1916–1918
HALDANE, John Reid	Surgeon-Lieutenant	Surgeon-Lieutenant-Commander	Royal Navy	Invalided, 1916	—	Gallipoli, 1915
HALLY, James D.	Lance-Corporal	Lance-Corporal	The Essex Regiment	Wounded, October 1917 and November 1917	—	France, 1917
HALLY, Peter	Lieutenant	Lieutenant	48th Canadian Highlanders	Wounded, April 1915 and July 1916	—	France, 1915–1916
HAMILTON, Alexander	Driver	Lieutenant	British Red Cross 5th Battn. The Cameronians (Scottish Rifles)	Wounded, July 1916	—	France, 1914–1916 and 1918
HAMILTON, Archibald Gordon	Cadet	Lieutenant	Royal Field Artillery	—	—	France, 1918

Name.	Rank. At beginning of War or on joining.	Rank. At end of War.	Unit.	Casualties.	Honours or Decorations.	Field of Service.
HAMILTON, Guy	Lieutenant	Commander	Royal Navy	—	—	—
HAMILTON, Robert J.	2nd Lieutenant	Lieutenant	Royal Field Artillery	—	—	—
✠ HARBOTTLE, Ian	2nd Lieutenant	Captain	Leicester Regiment	Killed in action, 21st March, 1918		France
HARDIE, David McA.	Driver	Driver	Royal Field Artillery	—		—
HARDIE, Gerald A.	Private	Lieutenant	The Cameronians (Scottish Rifles) The Royal Scots (Royal Regiment)	Invalided, March 1916	—	France, 1914–1916 West Africa, 1917–1918
HARDIE, John	Corporal	Corporal	5th Battn. The Cameronians (Scottish Rifles) Royal Engineers	Invalided, 1916	—	Home Service
HARKNESS, Joseph Welsh Park	Lieutenant	Major	Royal Army Medical Corps	Invalided, April 1916	Mentioned in Despatches twice	France, 1915–1916 Salonika, 1916–1918 Bulgaria, 1918
HARRINGTON, J. Wood	Engine-Room Artificer	Chief Warrant Engineer	Royal Naval Reserve	Invalided, 1916	—	At Sea, 1915–1918
HARRINGTON, Robert	Private	Private	14th London Regiment (London Scottish)	Wounded, 1916 Wounded, 1918	—	France, 1916 Salonika, 1916–1917 Palestine, 1917–1918

Name.	Rank. At beginning of War or on joining.	Rank. At end of War.	Unit.	Casualties.	Honours or Decorations.	Field of Service.
HART, Arthur Douglas	Captain	Major	5th Battn. The Cameronians (Scottish Rifles)	—	—	France, 1918
HARVEY, David	Major	Major-General	Royal Army Medical Corps	—	Mentioned in Despatches. Companion of the Order of the Bath. Companion of the Order of St. Michael and St. George. Commander of the Order of the British Empire	France and Belgium, 1914–1918
HARVEY, George H.	Lieutenant	Major	Royal Army Service Corps	—	—	—
HARVEY, George Thomson	Captain	Major	The Royal Scots (Royal Regiment)	Wounded, November 1916	—	Gallipoli, 1915. Egypt, 1916. France, 1916–1918
HARVEY, Gourlay	Captain	Captain	Calcutta Light Horse	—	—	—
HARVEY, James Robertson	Lieutenant-Commander	Commander	Royal Navy	—	Officer of the Order of the British Empire	At Sea, 1914–1918
HARVEY, Kenneth R.	Private	Lieutenant	17th Battn. Highland Light Infantry. The Loyal North Lancashire Regiment Machine Gun Corps	Wounded, July 1916. Wounded, November 1916	—	France, 1915–1918

Name.	Rank. At beginning of War or on joining.	Rank. At end of War.	Unit.	Casualties.	Honours or Decorations.	Field of Service.
HARVEY, Robert	Cadet	Cadet	Glasgow University Officers Training Corps	—	—	Home Service
✠ HARVEY, Thomas	Private	2nd Lieutenant	1st Rhodesian Regiment The King's Own Royal Lancaster Regiment	Died on active service, April 1916	—	German West African Campaign, 1915 Mesopotamia, 1916
HAWKE, Arthur George	Cadet	Sub-Lieutenant	Royal Navy	—	—	—
HAY, Archibald Gilchrist	Lieut.-Colonel	Lieut.-Colonel	Royal Army Medical Corps	Invalided, December 1918	Serbian Order of Saint Sava, 3rd Class	Salonika, 1916–1918
✠ HAYMAN, William Muir	Captain	Major	Royal Engineers	Wounded, August 1916 Died of wounds, 13th July, 1917	Mentioned in Despatches twice Distinguished Service Order	France, 1915–1917
HEDDERWICK, Arthur Stuart	Captain	Captain	General List	Invalided, 1918	Mentioned in Despatches twice	France, 1915–1918
HEDDERWICK, Robert J.	Cadet	2nd Lieutenant	Edinburgh University Officers Training Corps Scots Guards	—	—	—
✠ HENDERSON, George Gartly	2nd Lieutenant	2nd Lieutenant	17th Battn. Highland Light Infantry	Killed in action, 6th August, 1916	—	France, 1916
✠ HENDERSON, Hugo Fraser	Private	Sergeant	Royal Irish Rifles	Killed in action, 15th October, 1918	—	France

Name.	Rank. At beginning of War or on joining.	Rank. At end of War.	Unit.	Casualties.	Honours or Decorations.	Field of Service.
HENDERSON, J. Douglas	2nd Lieutenant	2nd Lieutenant	Royal Field Artillery	—	—	Belgium and France, 1915–1917
HENDERSON, James Arthur Fraser	Captain	Captain	Royal Flying Corps Royal Air Force	—	—	France, 1918
HENDERSON, William Boyd	Private	Private	Royal Army Service Corps	—	—	Mesopotamia, 1915
✠ HENDERSON-BEGG Robert	Captain	Major	Royal Garrison Artillery	Killed in action, 24th December, 1915, at Kut-el-Amara	—	France, 1916 East Africa, 1916–1918
HENDRY, Hamish G.	Private	Lieutenant	17th Battn. Highland Light Infantry 10th/11th Battn. Highland Light Infantry	Wounded, June 1916 Wounded, July 1917	—	—
HENDRY, James Walter	Cadet	2nd Lieutenant	Royal Garrison Artillery	—	—	France, 1918
HENRY, Herbert A.	2nd Lieutenant	Captain	7th Battn. Highland Light Infantry	—	Belgian War Cross	France, 1914–1918
HENRY, Ian M.	Private	Lieutenant	9th (G.H.) Battn. Highland Light Infantry	Wounded twice	Military Cross	—
HENRY, Ronald Robert	Private	Private	7th Battn. Highland Light Infantry Army Service Corps	—	—	—

Name.	Rank. At beginning of War or on joining.	Rank. At end of War.	Unit.	Casualties.	Honours or Decorations.	Field of Service.
HERBERTSON, George Richmond	2nd Lieutenant	Captain	8th Battn. The Cameronians (Scottish Rifles)	Wounded, March 1918	Mentioned in Despatches	France, 1916-1918
HERBERTSON, John Richmond	Lieutenant	Captain	Royal Army Medical Corps	—	—	France, 1917-1918
HERRIOT, William Maxwell	Private	Lieutenant	9th (G.H.) Battn. Highland Light Infantry	Wounded, February 1915 Wounded, September 1916	—	France, 1915-1918
✠ HERVIEU, Andre	Private	Sergeant-Major	French Army	Killed in action, 13th December, 1914	—	France, 1914
HEWAT, John Parker Douglas	2nd Lieutenant	Captain	9th (G.H.) Battn. Highland Light Infantry	Wounded, February 1915 Wounded, July 1916	—	France, 1914-1916 India and North West Frontier, 1917-1918
HIGGINBOTHAM, Herbert C.	2nd Lieutenant	Captain	3rd Battn. Argyll & Sutherland Highlanders Royal Flying Corps Royal Air Force	Wounded, April 1916 Wounded, August 1917	—	France, 1915-1917
HIGGINS, William	2nd Lieutenant	2nd Lieutenant	Armoured Cars The Lancashire Fusiliers	Wounded, August 1919	—	East Africa, 1916-1917 North Russia, 1918
HODGE, David C.	Private	Private	Lovat Scouts	—	—	—
HOGG, Alexander Kennedy Gibson	Private	Private	Sindh Rifles	—	—	—

NAME.	RANK. At beginning of War or on joining.	RANK. At end of War.	UNIT.	CASUALTIES.	HONOURS OR DECORATIONS.	FIELD OF SERVICE.
✚ HOGG, James Gordon	Private	Private	9th (G.H.) Battn. Highland Light Infantry	Invalided, December 1916 Died, January 1917	—	France, 1916
✚ HOLLIS, Basil	Lieutenant	Lieutenant	4/5th Battn. The Black Watch (Royal Highlanders)	Gassed, February 1917 Killed in action, 31st July, 1917	—	France, 1916–1917
HOLLIS, Guy Denzil	Captain	Major	Queen's Own Royal Glasgow Yeomanry	Invalided, November 1917 and May 1918	Mentioned in Despatches	France, 1918
HOLM, Andrew Mackie	2nd Lieutenant	Captain	5th Battn. Royal Scots Fusiliers	Invalided, March 1917 Wounded, October 1918	—	France, 1916–1917 Palestine, 1917–1918 France, 1918
✚ HOLMS, William	2nd Lieutenant	2nd Lieutenant	10/11th Battn. Highland Light Infantry	Killed in action, 16th September, 1916	—	France, 1916
✚ HOOD, John	2nd Lieutenant	Lieutenant	Argyll & Sutherland Highlanders Royal Flying Corps	Killed in action, 17th August, 1917	—	France
HOPKIN, Hugo L.	Sapper	Lieutenant	Royal Engineers 8th Battn. The Cameronians (Scottish Rifles)	Wounded	—	France, 1916–1917
HOPKIN, Robert	Sapper	Sapper	Royal Engineers	Invalided	—	—
HOTCHKIS, James Napier	Captain	Captain	Highland Cyclist Battn. Royal Field Artillery Highland Light Infantry	—	—	France and Belgium, 1915–1916 Malta, 1917–1918

NAME.	RANK. At beginning of War or on joining.	RANK. At end of War.	UNIT.	CASUALTIES.	HONOURS OR DECORATIONS.	FIELD OF SERVICE.
HOTCHKIS, R. D.	Major	Lieut.-Colonel	Royal Army Medical Corps	—	—	Home Service
HOTCHKIS, Richard James	2nd Lieutenant	Lieutenant	Highland Cyclist Battn.	—	—	France, 1915
HOUSTON, James	Private	2nd Lieutenant	Highland Light Infantry The Cameronians (Scottish Rifles)	—	—	—
HOWIE, Tom Osborne	2nd Lieutenant	Lieutenant	12th Battn. The Cameronians (Scottish Rifles)	—	—	Gallipoli, 1915; Serbia, 1915; Salonika, 1916–1917
HUME, W. Leslie	Private	Lance-Corporal	6th Battn. Highland Light Infantry Scottish Red Cross Mobile Unit	—	—	France, 1916–1918
HUNTER, General Sir Archibald, G.C.B.,G.C.V.O. D.S.O.	General	General	Staff	—	Legion of Honour, 2nd Class	Home Service
HUNTER, Douglas Macinnes	Major	Major	Royal Army Medical Corps	—	Mentioned in Despatches twice; Military Cross	France, 1914–1918
HUNTER, Eric Arrol	Sub-Lieutenant	Major	Royal Naval Volunteer Reserve; Royal Naval Air Service; Royal Air Force	—	Officer of the Order of the British Empire; Order of the Crown of Italy; Order of St. Ann; Order of St. Stanislaus	Armenia and Roumania, 1915–1917; Mediterranean, 1918

NAME.	RANK. At beginning of War or on joining.	RANK. At end of War.	UNIT.	CASUALTIES.	HONOURS OR DECORATIONS.	FIELD OF SERVICE.
HUNTER, G. G.	Captain	Brigadier-General	East Kent Regiment	—	Mentioned in Despatches. Companion of the Order of St. Michael and St. George. Companion of the Order of the Bath	Egypt, 1914–1918
HUNTER, Harold Clarke	Lieutenant	Lieutenant	11th Battery Motor Machine Guns	Gassed, April 1916	—	France, 1915–1916
HUNTER, John Miller	Captain	Captain	Royal Army Chaplains Department	Wounded, March 1918	Military Cross	France and Belgium, 1917–1918
HUNTER, Kenneth K.	Cadet	Cadet	Royal Navy	—	—	—
HUNTER, Norman Irwin	Captain	Major	15th Battn. Highland Light Infantry	Wounded, July 1916	Order of the Crown of Italy 4th Class. Brevet Major	France, 1915–1916
HUNTER, Ronald Galbraith	Gunner	Bombardier	Royal Field Artillery	—	—	—
HUNTER, Stuart Kerr	Private	Soldat	Royal Army Service Corps. French Army	Invalided out, 1915. Invalided out, 1918	—	France, 1917–1918
HUNTER, W. J. Harcourt	Lieutenant	Lieutenant	Royal Naval Volunteer Reserve	—	—	At Sea, 1917–1918
HUNTER, Walter K.	Major	Major	Royal Army Medical Corps	Invalided, March 1917–June 1917	—	Home Service

Name.	Rank. At beginning of War or on joining.	Rank. At end of War.	Unit.	Casualties.	Honours or Decorations.	Field of Service.
HUTSON, Guybon John	2nd Lieutenant	2nd Lieutenant	11th Battn. Gordon Highlanders	Wounded, October 1916	—	France, 1916
HUTSON, Thomas	2nd Lieutenant	Captain	King's Own Scottish Borderers	—	—	France, 1917–1918
✠ HUTTON, Frederick Robert Hughes	Lieutenant	Lieutenant	9th Battn. Argyll & Sutherland Highlanders	Killed in action, 10th May, 1915, at Ypres	—	France, 1915
HUTTON, George	2nd Lieutenant	Lieutenant	2nd Battn. The Royal Scots (Royal Regiment)	Wounded, April 1917	—	France and Belgium, 1917
INGLIS, Alexander	2nd Lieutenant	Major	4th Battn. Royal Scots Fusiliers	—	—	Gallipoli, Egypt, Palestine, 1915–1918
✠ INGLIS, David	Lieutenant	Captain	1/4th Gurkha Rifles	Killed in action, 19th December, 1914	—	France, 1914
INNES, Frederick	Private	Lieutenant	5th Battn. The Cameronians (Scottish Rifles)	Wounded, July 1916; Wounded, October 1917	—	France and Belgium, 1914–1917
INNES, Gilbert James	Captain	Captain	9th (G.H.) Battn. Highland Light Infantry; 8th Battn. The Cameronians (Scottish Rifles)	Wounded, July 1918	—	Egypt, Palestine, France, 1916–1918
INNES, John Richmond	Private	Captain	9th (G.H.) Battn. Highland Light Infantry; 8th Battn. The Cameronians (Scottish Rifles) Royal Engineers		Mentioned in Despatches	France, 1916–1918

NAME.	RANK. At beginning of War or on joining.	RANK. At end of War.	UNIT.	CASUALTIES.	HONOURS OR DECORATIONS.	FIELD OF SERVICE.
INNES, Thomas Richmond	Private	Private	5th Battn. The Cameronians (Scottish Rifles)	Wounded, April 1917. Prisoner of War, April 1918–November 1918	Military Medal	France, 1914–1916 and 1918. Salonika, 1916–1917
JACK, Thomas	Cadet	Cadet	Glasgow University Officers Training Corps	—	—	—
JACKSON, Alan Stewart	Gentleman-Cadet	Lieutenant	Royal Military College, Sandhurst. 2nd Battn. The Royal Scots (Royal Regiment)	Wounded, November 1916	Mentioned in Despatches	France, 1916
✠ JACKSON, Andrew Bain	Gunner	Gunner	Motor Machine Gun Corps	Invalided and died, 1917	—	Home Service
✠ JACKSON, George	2nd Lieutenant	Captain	9th (G.H.) Battn. Highland Light Infantry. 18th Battn. Highland Light Infantry	Killed in action, 25th August, 1917	—	France, 1914–1917
JACKSON, William Morrison	Private	Lieutenant	6th Battn. Highland Light Infantry. 6th Battn. South Staffordshire Regiment	Wounded, July 1915. Invalided, August 1916	—	Gallipoli, 1915. Egypt, 1916. France, 1917
✠ JARDINE, Graham Brymner	2nd Lieutenant	2nd Lieutenant	13th Battn. Argyll & Sutherland Highlanders	Invalided, June/August, 1916. Killed in action, 18th October, 1916, at Butte-de-Warlincourt	—	France, 1916

NAME.	RANK. At beginning of War or on joining.	RANK. At end of War.	UNIT.	CASUALTIES.	HONOURS OR DECORATIONS.	FIELD OF SERVICE.
JARDINE, Robin I.	Volunteer Driver	Volunteer Driver	Croix Rouge Française Section Sanitaire Anglaise 20	—	—	France, 1918
✠ JEBB, Arthur Beresford	Private	Lieutenant	14th London Regiment (London Scottish) Royal Field Artillery	Wounded, October 1915 Killed in action, 17th June, 1916	—	France, September 1914–1916
JENKINS, Leslie R. G.	Private	Lieutenant	5th Battn. Queen's Own Cameron Highlanders	Wounded, September 1915 Wounded, November 1917	Military Cross	France, 1915–1917
✠ JENKINS, Patrick Graham	Private	2nd Lieutenant	Calcutta Scottish Queen's Own Cameron Highlanders	Killed in action, 9th April, 1917	—	France, 1916–1917
JENKINS, Walter Hope Graham	2nd Lieutenant	Captain	7th Battn. Highland Light Infantry	—	—	Egypt, Palestine, France, 1916–1918
JOHANSON, J. Ferdinand	Private	Lance-Corporal	9th (G.H.) Battn. The Highland Light Infantry	Wounded, 1918	—	France, 1918
JOHANSON, J. Lauritz	Captain	Major	1st Battn. 7th Gurkha Rifles, Indian Army	—	3rd Class Order of The Star of Nepal	India
JOHNSTON, Dugald	Private	Sergeant	Motor Machine-Gun Training Centre	—	—	—
JOHNSTON, John Watson	Despatch Rider	Corporal	Royal Engineers	—	—	—

Name	Rank. At beginning of War or on joining.	Rank. At end of War.	Unit.	Casualties.	Honours or Decorations.	Field of Service.
✠ JOHNSTON, Robert Neilson	2nd Lieutenant	2nd Lieutenant	The Cameronians (Scottish Rifles)	Killed in action, 22nd July, 1916	—	France
JOHNSTON, Samuel S.	Private	Corporal	51st Battn. Highland Light Infantry	—	—	Army of Occupation
JOHNSTON, Thomas	2nd Lieutenant	2nd Lieutenant	Queen's Own Cameron Highlanders	—	—	Home Service
JOHNSTON, William Watson	Chaplain	Chaplain 4th Class	Royal Army Chaplains Department	—	—	France, 1916 and 1918
JOHNSTONE, Alexander S.	Trooper	Sergeant	Scottish Horse	—	—	—
JOHNSTONE, Douglas	Private	Private	Royal Army Service Corps	—	—	—
JOHNSTONE, George	Private	2nd Lieutenant	Highland Light Infantry Royal Scots Fusiliers	—	—	—
JOHNSTONE, James Spiers	Private	Captain	Royal Fusiliers Middlesex Regiment	Invalided, 1916 Wounded, November 1917	—	Egypt, 1915–1916 France, 1916 Palestine, 1917–1918
JOHNSTONE, Peter A. S.	Trooper	Squadron Sergeant Major	Scottish Horse	—	—	—
✠ JONES, Arthur Meredydd	Private	Captain	Royal Army Medical Corps 17th Battn. Durham Light Infantry Machine Gun Corps	Wounded, 1916 Wounded, 1918 twice Wounded and missing, 10th April, 1918	Military Cross Bar to Military Cross	France, 1915–1918

Name.	Rank. At beginning of War or on joining.	Rank. At end of War.	Unit.	Casualties.	Honours or Decorations.	Field of Service.
Jones, Ellis	Lieutenant	Lieutenant	Royal Field Artillery	—	—	—
Kay, Alexander	Private	Private	28th (County of London) Battn. The London Regiment (Artists Rifles)	—	—	Home Service
Kay, John Robert	Private	Lieutenant	14th Battn. Argyll & Sutherland Highlanders	Prisoner of War, December 1916	—	France, 1916
Kay, William Martin	Lieut.-Colonel	Colonel	6th Battn. The Cameronians (Scottish Rifles)	Wounded, June 1915	Mentioned in Despatches Companion of the Order of St. Michael and St. George	France 1915–1916
Kellock, David	Corporal	Corporal	9th (G.H.) Battn. Highland Light Infantry Gordon Highlanders	—	—	France and Belgium, 1916–1918
Kellock, James	Private	Private	Royal Army Medical Corps	—	—	France, 1915 Salonika, 1915–1918
✠ Kelly, Thomas Cameron	2nd Lieutenant	2nd Lieutenant	16th Battn. Highland Light Infantry	Killed in action, March 1916	—	France, 1916
Kelly, William Thomson	2nd Lieutenant	Captain	15th Battn. Highland Light Infantry	—	Military Cross	France and Belgium, 1916–1918
✠ Kennedy, Duncan Cameron	2nd Lieutenant	Lieutenant	9th (G.H.) Battn. Highland Light Infantry	Killed in action, 9th September, 1916, at Guinchy	—	Flanders, 1916

NAME.	RANK. At beginning of War or on joining.	RANK. At end of War.	UNIT.	CASUALTIES.	HONOURS OR DECORATIONS.	FIELD OF SERVICE.
KENNEDY, Hugh	2nd Lieutenant	2nd Lieutenant	Royal Scots Fusiliers	—	Military Cross	—
KENNEDY, James G.	Cadet	2nd Lieutenant	Royal Flying Corps Royal Air Force	—	—	—
KENNEDY, W. W.	Captain	Captain	Calcutta Rifle Volunteers	—	—	—
KENNEDY, William R.	2nd Lieutenant	2nd Lieutenant	Royal Scots Fusiliers	Wounded	—	—
KENNETH, John Henry	Private	Private	Royal Army Medical Corps	—	—	France, 1915–1918
KER, Hugh Torrance	2nd Lieutenant	Major	17th Battn. Northumberland Fusiliers	—	Mentioned in Despatches Officer of the Order of the British Empire	France, 1915–1917
KERR, Cyril A.	Private	Private	Training Reserve Battn.	Wounded	—	—
KERR, Gordon	Captain	Captain	7th Battn. The Cameronians (Scottish Rifles)	Invalided, June 1916 Wounded, April 1917	—	Egypt, 1916 France, 1917 Palestine, 1917–1918 France, 1918
KERR, J. H., C.I.E.,	Private	Private	Calcutta Scottish	—	—	—
KERR, James	Lieutenant	Captain	Royal Garrison Artillery	—	—	—

NAME.	RANK. At beginning of War or on joining.	RANK. At end of War.	UNIT.	CASUALTIES.	HONOURS OR DECORATIONS.	FIELD OF SERVICE.
KIDD, James Dunlop	Captain	Lieut.-Colonel	Royal Army Medical Corps	—	Mentioned in Despatches twice. Officer of the Order of the British Empire. Military Cross. Brevet Major	East Africa, 1914–1918
KILPATRICK, Alexander Watt	2nd Lieutenant	2nd Lieutenant	Royal Air Force	Wounded, October 1918	—	France, 1918
KILPATRICK, Daniel Ross	Lieutenant	Major	Royal Army Medical Corps	Invalided, September 1915	—	Gallipoli, 1915
KING, Norris W.	Cadet	Cadet	Glasgow University Officers Training Corps	—	—	Home Service
KING, Walter	Lieutenant	Lieutenant	Queen's Own Royal Glasgow Yeomanry	—	—	—
KINGHORN, David	Private	Lieutenant	The Border Regiment	Invalided, April 1917; Wounded, April 1918	—	France, 1917–1918
KINLOCH, Henry Taylor	2nd Lieutenant	Captain	6th Battn. Highland Light Infantry	Prisoner of War, March–December 1918	—	France, 1917–1918
✠ KINLOCH, James Moncrieff Thomson	Private	Lieutenant	9th (G.H.) Battn. Highland Light Infantry. Royal Engineers	Killed in action, 11th/12th July, 1915	—	France, 1914–1915
KINLOCH, John A.	Lieutenant	Lieutenant	Royal Naval Volunteer Reserve	—	—	—

NAME.	RANK. At beginning of War on joining.	RANK. At end of War.	UNIT.	CASUALTIES.	HONOURS OR DECORATIONS.	FIELD OF SERVICE.
KINLOCH, Peter Stewart	Private	Private	17th Battn. Highland Light Infantry	Wounded, 1916	—	France, 1915–1916
KINLOCH, William	Private	Captain	9th Hodsons Horse (Indian Army)	—	—	Indian Frontier, 1915–1916; France, 1916–1918; Palestine and Syria, 1918
KIRKPATRICK, Hubert V.	Lieutenant	Lieutenant	Royal Artillery	—	—	Belgium, 1915; Egypt, Palestine, Syria, 1916–1918
KIRKWOOD, John E. H.	Private	2nd Lieutenant	Australian Army Service Corps	—	—	—
KIRSOP, Conrad R. J.	Lieutenant	Lieutenant	Royal Field Artillery	—	—	—
KIRSOP, John	Private	Lieutenant	Royal Army Service Corps	—	—	Home Service
KIRSOP, Purves Alexander	Lieutenant	Major	9th Battn. Argyll & Sutherland Highlanders	Injured in Gretna Railway Disaster 1915	Mentioned in Despatches; Military Cross; Bar to Military Cross	France, 1915 and 1918
KUTTNER, Edgar Harold	Private	Private	Royal Army Service Corps King's African Rifles	—	—	East Africa, 1916–1918
✠ LAIDLAW, Andrew Hunter	Private	Private	5th Battn. Queen's Own Cameron Highlanders	Missing, 25th September, 1915, at Battle of Loos	—	France, 1915

NAME.	RANK. At beginning of War or on joining.	RANK. At end of War.	UNIT.	CASUALTIES.	HONOURS OR DECORATIONS.	FIELD OF SERVICE.
LAIDLAW, Henry	Private	Private	5th Battn. Queen's Own Cameron Highlanders	Wounded, November 1915	—	France, 1915
LAING, A. R.	Captain	Major	7th Battn. Highland Light Infantry	—	—	—
✠ LAIRD, Arthur Donald	Private	Lieutenant	17th Battn. Highland Light Infantry	Killed in action, 1st July, 1916, at Battle of the Somme	—	France, 1915-1916
LAIRD, George	Private	Sergeant	Royal Army Medical Corps; 1st Battn. The Seaforth Highlanders	Invalided, December 1916; Invalided, December 1917	—	Mediterranean, 1915-1916; Mesopotamia, 1916-1917; Syria, 1918
LAIRD, George Donald Struthers	Cadet	Company Sergeant Major	Glasgow University Officers Training Corps	—	—	Home Service
LAIRD, George Holms Reid	Lieutenant	Captain	6th Battn. Highland Light Infantry	Wounded, July 1915	—	Gallipoli, 1915
LAIRD, W. W.	Lieutenant	Major	Royal Artillery	—	Order of the Nile, 4th Class	Egypt and Palestine, 1916-1918
✠ LAKEMAN, Harold Leslie	Private	2nd Lieutenant	28th (County of London) Battn. The London Regiment (Artist's Rifles) Army Service Corps	Killed in action, 23rd August, 1918	—	France, 1915-1918
✠ LAMONT, James Kenneth	2nd Lieutenant	Lieutenant	Royal Field Artillery	Invalided, January 1916; Killed in action, 27th October, 1917	—	Suvla Bay, 1915; France and Flanders, 1917

Name.	Rank. At beginning of War or on joining.	At end of War.	Unit.	Casualties.	Honours or Decorations.	Field of Service.
LAMONT, Lewis Norman	2nd Lieutenant	2nd Lieutenant	Royal Field Artillery	—	—	France and Belgium, 1917–1918
LAMONT, William	Lieutenant-Colonel	Lieutenant-Colonel	Royal Field Artillery	—	—	France
✠ LANG, Arthur	2nd Lieutenant	Lieutenant	6th Battn. Argyll & Sutherland Highlanders	Killed in action, 29th August, 1916	—	France, 1915
✠ LANG, Frederick Murray	Lieutenant	Captain	6th Battn. Argyll & Sutherland Highlanders	Died of wounds, 18th December, 1915	—	France, 1914–1915
✠ LANG, Hugh Muir	Private	Private	9th (G.H.) Battn. Highland Light Infantry	Killed in action, 14th February, 1915	—	France, 1915
LANG, James O.	2nd Lieutenant	Lieutenant	6th Battn. Argyll & Sutherland Highlanders	Wounded, 1915	—	France, 1918
LANG, Laurence Russell	Private	Lieutenant	Royal Flying Corps Royal Air Force	—	—	—
LANG, W. Douglas	2nd Lieutenant	2nd Lieutenant	Argyll & Sutherland Highlanders	—	—	France and Belgium, 1917
LAUDER, Douglas Munro	2nd Lieutenant	2nd Lieutenant	Manchester Regiment	Wounded, 1917	—	France and Belgium, 1915–1918
LAURIE, George Vernon	Lieutenant	Lieutenant	6th Battn. The Cameronians (Scottish Rifles) 4th (City of London) Battn. The London Regiment (Royal Fusiliers)	—	Mentioned in Despatches Military Cross	

Name.	Rank. At beginning of War or on joining.	Rank. At end of War.	Unit.	Casualties.	Honours or Decorations.	Field of Service.
LAW, Andrew	Lieutenant	Captain	Argyll & Sutherland Highlanders	Wounded, November 1917 Wounded, August 1918	—	France, 1916–1918
LAW, Harold B.	Lieutenant	Major	Queen's Own Cameron Highlanders	—	—	France
LAW, Robert A.	2nd Lieutenant	2nd Lieutenant	Argyll & Sutherland Highlanders	—	—	—
LAW, William Ramsay	2nd Lieutenant	Captain	7th Battn. The Cameronians (Scottish Rifles)	Invalided, January 1916	Military Cross	Gallipoli, 1915–1916 Sinai and Palestine, 1917–1918 France, 1918
✠ LAWRIE, Allan James	Lieutenant	Captain	6th Battn. The Cameronians (Scottish Rifles)	Killed in action, 16th May, 1915, at Laventie	—	France, 1915
LAWRIE, Frank W. K.	Lieutenant	Captain	Royal Army Medical Corps	—	Military Cross	France, 1917 Italy, 1917 France, 1918
LAWRIE, Walter C.	Colonel	Colonel	Royal Engineers	—	—	—
LEAN, William Kennedy	Conducteur Driver of Ambulance	Conducteur Driver of Ambulance	Section Sanitaire Anglaise No. 20 French Red Cross	Gassed, February 1916	French War Cross	France, 1915–1918
LEASK, Lewis White	Sub-Lieutenant	Sub-Lieutenant	Royal Navy	—	—	—
LECKIE, D. J.	Trooper	Trooper	Calcutta Light Horse	—	—	India

Name.	Rank. At beginning of War or on joining.	Rank. At end of War.	Unit.	Casualties.	Honours or Decorations.	Field of Service.
Lee, Walter E.	Chaplain 4th Class	Chaplain 3rd Class	Royal Army Chaplains Department	Invalided, December 1915	—	Gallipoli, 1915 Egypt, 1916 France and Belgium, 1916 Italy, 1918
Legate, Alistair B. S.	Private	Lieutenant	Royal Fusiliers Argyll & Sutherland Highlanders Cameron Highlanders	—	—	France
✠ Legate, Francis	2nd Lieutenant	Lieutenant	5th Battn. The Highland Light Infantry	Killed in action, 27th August, 1918, at Fontaine Crosilles	—	France
Leys, Herbert H.	2nd Lieutenant	Lieutenant	Royal Field Artillery Royal Engineers	Wounded, 1917 Invalided	—	Egypt, 1915–1916 Salonica, 1916–1917
Lightbody, Ivan Stuart	Sapper	2nd Lieutenant	Royal Engineers	—	—	France and Belgium, 1917–1918
Lightbody, William T.	Private	Private	9th (G.H.) Battn. Highland Light Infantry	Invalided	—	France, 1914–1916
✠ Lindsay, Douglas Alexander Bowman	Private	2nd Lieutenant	Highland Light Infantry 10th Battn. The Cameronians (Scottish Rifles)	Killed in action, 24th September, 1915, at Loos	—	France, 1915
Lindsay, Ronald Hewes	Private	Private	—	—	—	—
Lindsay, W. G. O.	Private	Captain	9th (G.H.) Battn. Highland Light Infantry	—	—	Home Service

Name.	Rank. At beginning of War or on joining.	Rank. At end of War.	Unit.	Casualties.	Honours or Decorations.	Field of Service.
LITHGOW, Sir James, Bt.	Captain	Lieut. Colonel	Royal Garrison Artillery	Wounded, May 1917	Mentioned in Despatches Military Cross Brevet Lieut.-Colonel	France, 1916-1917
LOCHHEAD, R. Norman	Lieutenant	Lieutenant	Royal Field Artillery	—	Military Cross	France, 1918
LOUDON, John	Lieutenant	Captain	8th Battn. The Cameronians (Scottish Rifles)	—	—	—
LOW, Duncan Whyte	Lieutenant	Lieutenant	Royal Naval Volunteer Reserve	—	—	North Sea Patrol, 1914-1915 Channel Patrol, 1916 Mediterranean Patrol, 1916-1917 Atlantic Patrol, 1917-1918
✠ LOWSON, Norman Coutie	2nd Lieutenant	Captain	Royal Engineers	Died of wounds, 6th March, 1917, at Puisieux	Mentioned in Despatches three times Military Cross	France, 1914-1917
LYLE, James A.	Captain	Captain	7th Battn. Highland Light Infantry	Invalided, September 1915 June 1916	Mentioned in Despatches	Gallipoli, 1915 Egypt, 1916-1918 France and Belgium, 1918
McALISTER, Angus	Lieutenant	Major	Royal Engineers,	Wounded, December 1914	Mentioned in Despatches Order of St. Maurice and St. Lazarus, 5th Class	France, 1914

VICTORIA CROSS

" For most conspicuous bravery, determination, and gallant leading of his command. The enemy attacked on the right of the battalion frontage, and succeeded in penetrating the Wood held by our men. Owing to successive lines of the enemy following on closely there was the gravest danger that the flank of the whole position would be turned. Grasping the seriousness of the situation Colonel Anderson made his way across the open in full view of the enemy now holding the Wood on the right, and after much effort succeeded in gathering the remainder of the two right companies. He personally led the counter attack and drove the enemy from the Wood, capturing twelve machine guns and 70 prisoners, and restoring the original line. His conduct in leading the charge was quite fearless, and his most splendid example was the means of rallying and inspiring the men during the most critical hour.

" Later on the same day in another position, the enemy had penetrated to within 300 yards of the village and were holding a timber yard in force. Colonel Anderson reorganised his men after they had been driven in and brought them forward to a position of readiness for a counter attack. He led the attack in person and throughout shewed the utmost disregard for his own safety. The counter attack drove the enemy from his position but resulted in this very gallant officer losing his life. He died fighting within the enemy lines, setting a magnificent example to all who were privileged to serve under him ".

LIEUTENANT-COLONEL WILLIAM HERBERT ANDERSON V.C.

HIGHLAND LIGHT INFANTRY

KILLED IN ACTION 25TH MARCH 1918

Name.	Rank. At beginning of War or on joining.	At end of War.	Unit.	Casualties.	Honours or Decorations.	Field of Service.
✠ MACALISTER, William Grierson	Captain	Major	5th Battn. The Cameronians (Scottish Rifles)	Killed in action, 20th July, 1916	Mentioned in Despatches twice	France, 1914–1916
MACARTHUR, John McLachlan	Private	Lieutenant	Highland Light Infantry	Wounded, July 1916 Invalided, October 1917	—	France, 1916–1917
MACARTHUR, Roy	Private	Captain	28th (County of London) Battn. The London Regiment (Artists Rifles)	—	—	France, 1918–1919
MACBEAN, Aeneas Allison	Major	Major	Royal Engineers	—	—	Home Service
MACBETH, John Douglas	Private	2nd Lieutenant	Highland Light Infantry	Wounded	—	—
✠ MACBETH, J. D. G.	2nd Lieutenant	Lieutenant	5th Battn. Highland Light Infantry Royal Scots Fusiliers	Wounded and missing, 1917	—	Egypt, 1917
MACBETH, W. G.	2nd Lieutenant	2nd Lieutenant	9th (G.H.) Battn. Highland Light Infantry	—	—	—
MACBRAYNE, Alan Burns	Naval Cadet	Midshipman	Royal Navy	—	—	Black Sea
MACBRAYNE, David	2nd Lieutenant	Lieutenant	The Royal Scots (Royal Regiment)	Wounded	—	France, 1914 and 1917–1918 Egypt, 1915–1916
✠ MACBRAYNE, John Burns	2nd Lieutenant	Lieutenant	17th Battn. Highland Light Infantry	Killed in action, 1st July, 1916, at the Somme	—	France, 1915–1916
McCAIG, Robert W. L.	Lieutenant	Lieutenant	The Cameronians (Scottish Rifles)	Invalided, April 1917 Wounded, May 1918	—	France, 1916–1918

F

NAME.	RANK. At beginning of War or on joining.	RANK. At end of War.	UNIT.	CASUALTIES.	HONOURS OR DECORATIONS.	FIELD OF SERVICE.
McCALLUM, Hugh Gibson	Private	Captain	6th Battn. Argyll & Sutherland Highlanders 18th Battn. Highland Light Infantry	Wounded, October 1918	—	Mesopotamia and India, 1918
McCALLUM, John A.	Trooper	Trooper	Queen's Own Royal Glasgow Yeomanry	—	—	—
MacCONNELL, Archibald Laird	Captain	Major	9th Battn. Argyll & Sutherland Highlanders	Wounded, May 1915	Mentioned in Despatches three times Distinguished Service Order	France and Belgium, 1915–1918
MacCONNELL, George Herbert	Trooper	Lieutenant	3rd Scottish Horse	Wounded, May 1915 Invalided, June 1916	—	France, 1915
McCONNELL, William A. C.	2nd Lieutenant	Lieutenant	5th Battn. The Cameronians (Scottish Rifles)	Wounded, May 1917	—	France, 1917
McCORKINDALE, Ian Henry	Private	2nd Lieutenant	Queen's Own Cameron Highlanders King's Liverpool Regiment	—	—	—
✠ MACOUAT, John	Private	2nd Lieutenant	12th Battn. The Royal Scots (Royal Regiment)	Killed in action, 12th April, 1917, at Arras	—	France, 1916–1917
✠ McCOWAN, Hew	2nd Lieutenant	Lieutenant	8th Battn. The Cameronians (Scottish Rifles)	Killed in action, 28th June, 1915, at Cape Helles	—	Gallipoli, 1915
McCRACKEN, Arthur Dewar	Private	Lieutenant	Royal Garrison Artillery	—	—	Home Service

Name.	Rank. At beginning of War or on joining.	Rank. At end of War.	Unit.	Casualties.	Honours or Decorations.	Field of Service.
McCracken, James O.	2nd Lieutenant	Lieutenant	7th Battn. Argyll & Sutherland Highlanders	Wounded, July 1916	—	France, 1916
✠ McCrae, Alister Bisset	Private	Lieutenant	5th Battn. The Cameronians (Scottish Rifles)	Wounded, August 1917 Killed in action, September 1918	Military Cross	France, 1917–1918
McCrae, Donald	Corporal	Lieutenant	Royal Engineers King's African Rifles	—	—	—
McCrae, Jack	Private	Lieutenant	9th (G.H.) Battn. Highland Light Infantry 5th Battn. Argyll & Sutherland Highlanders	—	—	France, 1918
✠ Macrae, John Harold	2nd Lieutenant	2nd Lieutenant	The Cameronians (Scottish Rifles)	Killed in action, 26th August, 1916	—	France
Macrae, Norman R. M.	2nd Lieutenant	Lieutenant	The Cameronians (Scottish Rifles)	Wounded, July 1916 Wounded, October 1918	—	France, 1916 and 1918
✠ Macrae, William Charles McIntyre	Private	Captain	The London Regiment	Killed in action, 27th September, 1918	—	France
Macrae, William Donald	2nd Lieutenant	Captain	6th Battn. Highland Light Infantry	Wounded, 1917	Military Cross	Gallipoli, 1915–1916 Egypt and Palestine, 1915–1918 France and Belgium, 1918
Macrae, W. M.	2nd Lieutenant	Lieutenant	Royal Army Service Corps	—	—	—

Name.	Rank. At beginning of War or on joining.	Rank. At end of War.	Unit.	Casualties.	Honours or Decorations.	Field of Service.
McCrae, William R.	2nd Lieutenant	Captain	The Cameronians (Scottish Rifles)	—	Mentioned in Despatches	France, 1915–1917
McCrossan, Allan D.	Private	Lieutenant	5th Battn. Queen's Own Cameron Highlanders	Wounded, September 1915. Invalided, January 1919	—	France, 1915. India, 1917–1918
✠ McCulloch, George	Gunner	Gunner	15th Battery Canadian Field Artillery	Killed in action, 1st September, 1917	—	France, 1915–1917
McCulloch, John	Private	Lieutenant	Canadian Forces	—	Military Medal	—
✠ McCulloch, Norman	Private	Private	42nd Battn. (Infantry) Canadian Expeditionary Forces	Killed in action, 16th September, 1916	—	France, 1916
McCulloch, Richard	Gunner	Gunner	Canadian Forces	—	—	—
✠ McCulloch, Robert Patrick	Private	Private	5th Battn. Queen's Own Cameron Highlanders	Killed in action, 25th September, 1915	—	France, 1915
McCunn, John N.	Private	Private	Highland Light Infantry	—	—	—
McDiarmid, Charles R.	Private	Private	The Black Watch (Royal Highlanders)	—	—	—
MacDonald, Alan Blair	2nd Lieutenant	Captain	Royal Field Artillery	—	Mentioned in Despatches	France and Flanders, 1916–1917 and 1918. Italy, 1917–1918

NAME.	RANK. At beginning of War or on joining.	RANK. At end of War.	UNIT.	CASUALTIES.	HONOURS OR DECORATIONS.	FIELD OF SERVICE.
McDONALD, George	2nd Lieutenant	2nd Lieutenant	Highland Light Infantry	—	—	—
MACDONALD, George Fyfe	2nd Lieutenant	Captain	8th Battn. Highland Light Infantry	Invalided, February 1917	—	France, 1916–1917
✠ McDONALD, Harold Stewart	2nd Lieutenant	2nd Lieutenant	5th Battn. The Cameronians (Scottish Rifles)	Killed in action, 21st September, 1918, at Cambrai	—	France, 1918
MACDONALD, Hew Webster	2nd Lieutenant	Lieutenant	5th Battn. The Cameronians (Scottish Rifles)	Wounded, March 1917	—	France, 1916–1918
MACDONALD, Hugh Cameron	Captain	Major	5th Battn. Highland Light Infantry	—	—	France, 1917–1918
MACDONALD, J. K.	Private	Private	Queen's Own Cameron Highlanders	—	—	—
MACDONALD, John	Cadet	Cadet	Glasgow University Officers Training Corps	—	—	—
✠ MACDONALD, John	Captain	Captain	5th Battn. Highland Light Infantry	Killed in action, 12th July, 1915	Mentioned in Despatches	Gallipoli, 1915
✠ MACDONALD, Sydney	2nd Lieutenant	Lieutenant	The Royal Scots (Royal Regiment)	Killed in action, 2nd September, 1918	—	France
MACDONALD, Symington	2nd Lieutenant	Captain	3rd Battn. The Cameronians (Scottish Rifles)	Wounded, December 1915	Military Cross	Salonika, 1915 France, 1916
MACDONALD, Thomas Logie	Cadet	Cadet	Glasgow University Officers Training Corps	—	—	Home Service

Name.	Rank. At beginning of War or on joining.	Rank. At end of War.	Unit.	Casualties.	Honours or Decorations.	Field of Service.
MacDonald, Thomas Wilson	Major	Major	The Border Regiment	Wounded, June 1915	Mentioned in Despatches three times. Distinguished Service Order	France, 1914–1918
McDonald, William	Captain	Captain	4th Battn. Highland Light Infantry	Wounded, March 1916	Mentioned in Despatches	France, 1915–1916. Mesopotamia, 1916–1918
MacDougall, George Wallace	Private	Private	Queen's Own Cameron Highlanders	—	—	—
MacDougall, Thomas	Lance-Corporal	Lance-Corporal	Queen's Own Royal Glasgow Yeomanry	—	—	—
McEwan, Alan Douglas	Private	2nd Lieutenant	South African Mounted Rifles. Royal Field Artillery	Wounded	—	—
✠ MacEwan, George Lammie	Lieutenant	Captain	6th Battn. Highland Light Infantry	Died of wounds, 12th July, 1915	—	Gallipoli, 1915
MacFarlane, James	2nd Lieutenant	2nd Lieutenant	Royal Field Artillery	—	—	—
Macfarlane, James B.	Private	Lieutenant	14th London Regiment (London Scottish). Royal Field Artillery	Wounded, 1915	—	France and Belgium, 1914–1918
Macfarlane, James Golder	Private	Major	7th Battn. The Cameronians (Scottish Rifles)	Wounded, July 1915	Mentioned in Despatches	Gallipoli, 1915. Egypt and Palestine, 1916–1918

NAME.	RANK. At beginning of War or on joining.	RANK. At end of War.	UNIT.	CASUALTIES.	HONOURS OR DECORATIONS.	FIELD OF SERVICE.
✠ MACFARLANE, John Tennant	2nd Lieutenant	Lieutenant	Machine Gun Corps	Killed in action, 26th September, 1915	—	France, 1915
MACFARLANE, Robert S.	2nd Lieutenant	2nd Lieutenant	Highland Light Infantry	—	—	—
MACFARLANE, Thomas C.	Cadet	Cadet	Glasgow University Officers Training Corps	—	—	Home Service
MACFARLANE, Walter	Captain	Major	Queen's Own Royal Glasgow Yeomanry	—	Mentioned in Despatches three times; Distinguished Service Order; Italian War Cross	France, 1915–1918; Italy, 1918
McGAVIN, Colin McKenzie	Private	Major	17th Battn. Highland Light Infantry; Royal Scots Fusiliers; Royal Air Force	Wounded, August 1915; Wounded, September 1915	Mentioned in Despatches	France, 1915
McGAVIN, Lawrence Pursell	Private	Lieutenant	Royal Artillery	Invalided, May 1917	—	France and Belgium, 1918
McGAVIN, Nathan P.	Private	Lieutenant	17th Battn. Highland Light Infantry	Invalided, October 1916	—	France, 1916 and 1918
McGEE, Gilmour Brown	Lieutenant	Lieutenant	6th Battn. Argyll & Sutherland Highlanders	Wounded, March 1918	—	France, 1917–1918
MACGILL, John	2nd Lieutenant	Captain	9th Battn. Highland Light Infantry	—	—	Home Service

NAME.	RANK. At beginning of War or on joining.	RANK. At end of War.	UNIT.	CASUALTIES.	HONOURS OR DECORATIONS.	FIELD OF SERVICE.
MacGillivray, Hugh Edward	Private	2nd Lieutenant	Royal Army Service Corps	Injured, January 1916 Wounded, June 1918	—	France, 1915–1918
MacGregor, J. A.	2nd Lieutenant	2nd Lieutenant	Argyll & Sutherland Highlanders		Military Cross	—
✠ MacGregor, James Gregor	2nd Lieutenant	Lieutenant	Royal Field Artillery	Died on Service, 12th July, 1918	—	Egypt
MacGregor, John Francis	Private	Private	14th London Regiment (London Scottish)	—	—	Home Service
McIntosh, Douglas B.	Captain	Captain	Royal Army Medical Corps	—	—	Mesopotamia, 1916–1918
McIntosh, Gordon Thomson	Private	Lieutenant	5th Battn. Queen's Own Cameron Highlanders 6th Battn. Highland Light Infantry	Wounded, September 1915 Invalided, December 1916 Wounded, December 1917	Military Cross	France, 1915–1918
McIntyre, Robert McKay	Sapper	Sapper	Royal Engineers	—	—	—
Mackay, Alastair Moray	Lieutenant	Captain	9th (G.H.) Battn. Highland Light Infantry	Wounded, May 1915 Wounded, April 1918	—	France, 1914–1915 and 1917–1918
Mackay, Eric Bryce	2nd Lieutenant	2nd Lieutenant	Royal Garrison Artillery	—	—	Home Service
Mackay, Ian Aberigh	Private	Private	Highland Light Infantry	—	—	—

Name	Rank — At beginning of War or on joining	Rank — At end of War	Unit	Casualties	Honours or Decorations	Field of Service
✠ MACKAY, Ian Darroch	2nd Lieutenant	2nd Lieutenant	3rd Battn. Argyll & Sutherland Highlanders	Killed in action, March 1918	—	France, 1917–1918
✠ MACKAY, Ian Norman	Private	Private	9th (G.H.) Battn. Highland Light Infantry	Died on Service, 19th January, 1915	—	France, 1914–1915
MACKAY, John Martin	Private	Lieutenant	5th Battn. The Royal Scots (Royal Regiment)	—	—	France, 1918
✠ MACKAY, Norman M.	Private	Private	Seaforth Highlanders	Died of wounds, 1916	—	France
✠ MACKAY, Samuel Francis Henderson	Lieutenant	Captain	5th Battn. The East Lancashire Regiment	Died of wounds, June 1917	—	France, 1917
McKECHNIE, Charles James Dickson	Private	Private	5th Battn. The Royal Scots (Royal Regiment)	Wounded four times	—	Gallipoli, 1915 France, 1916–1918
✠ McKECHNIE, Robert J.	Private	Private	Royal Army Service Corps	Accidently killed, 22nd June, 1916	—	Home Service
McKENZIE, Alexander W.	2nd Lieutenant	2nd Lieutenant	Royal Scots Fusiliers	Wounded	—	—
MACKENZIE, Donald	2nd Lieutenant	2nd Lieutenant	King's Own Scottish Borderers	—	—	—
MACKENZIE, George	2nd Lieutenant	Lieutenant	Queen's Own Cameron Highlanders	—	—	—

Name.	Rank. At beginning of War or on joining.	Rank. At end of War.	Unit.	Casualties.	Honours or Decorations.	Field of Service.
MacKenzie, Sir Robert C., C.B.	Colonel	Colonel Commandant	3rd Line Lowland Division Chairman, Territorial Army Association of the County of the City of Glasgow	—	Mentioned in Despatches Knight Commander of the Order of the British Empire	Home Service
MacKichan, Edward W.	Lieut.-Commander	Commander	Royal Navy	—	—	At Sea, 1914–1917
MacKichan, Kenneth William	Private	Lieutenant	Royal Field Artillery	Wounded, February 1917 Wounded, September 1918	—	India, 1915–1916 Mesopotamia, 1916–1917 Egypt, 1918
MacKie, Robert Cuthbert	Cadet	2nd Lieutenant	Glasgow University Officers Training Corps Highland Light Infantry	—	—	—
MacKie, William G.	Orderly	Lance-Corporal	Motor Ambulance Argyll & Sutherland Highlanders	—	—	—
MacKinlay, Ian B.	Private	Lieutenant	5th Battn. The Cameronians (Scottish Rifles)	Gassed, November 1917	—	France and Belgium, 1917–1918
MacKinlay, Louis B.	Private	Lieutenant	Queen's Own Cameron Highlanders Royal Flying Corps	Wounded	—	France and Belgium
✠ MacKinnon, Andrew William	Private	Lieutenant	5th Battn. The Cameronians (Scottish Rifles)	Died, 14th October, 1918	—	France, 1914–1918

NAME.	RANK. At beginning of War or on joining.	RANK. At end of War.	UNIT.	CASUALTIES.	HONOURS OR DECORATIONS.	FIELD OF SERVICE.
MacKinnon, Osborne A.	2nd Lieutenant	2nd Lieutenant	Royal Field Artillery	—	—	—
McKinnon, Samuel Cockburn	2nd Lieutenant	Lieutenant	Queen's Own Cameron Highlanders	Invalided, September 1916; Gassed, September 1917	—	France, 1915–1917
✠ MacKinnon, Thomas Neill	Private	Private	Princess Patricia's Canadian Light Infantry	Wounded and missing, 2nd June, 1916	—	France, 1916
✠ Mackintosh, Donald	2nd Lieutenant	Lieutenant	Seaforth Highlanders	Killed in action, 11th April, 1917	Mentioned in Despatches; Victoria Cross	France
✠ MacKissock, William B.	Private	Company Quarter-Master Sergeant	Canadian Forces	Killed in action, 9th April, 1917	Military Medal	France
✠ Maclay, Ebenezer	2nd Lieutenant	2nd Lieutenant	8th Battn. The Cameronians (Scottish Rifles); Scots Guards	Invalided, 1915; Died of wounds, 11th April, 1918	—	Gallipoli, 1915; France, 1918
✠ Maclay, J. W.	2nd Lieutenant	2nd Lieutenant	The Cameronians (Scottish Rifles)	Missing	—	—
✠ Maclay, William Strang	2nd Lieutenant	2nd Lieutenant	8th Battn. The Cameronians (Scottish Rifles)	Killed in action, 28th June, 1915, in Gallipoli	—	Gallipoli, 1915
Maclean, John M.	Private	Private	The Cameronians (Scottish Rifles)	Wounded	Distinguished Conduct Medal	France

Name.	Rank. At beginning of War or on joining.	Rank. At end of War.	Unit.	Casualties.	Honours or Decorations.	Field of Service.
McLELLAN, Archibald	Cadet	Sergeant	Edinburgh University Officers Training Corps	—	—	Home Service
✠ McLELLAND, Archibald	Private	Private	Lovat's Scouts	Died of wounds, 10th April, 1917	—	France, 1916–1917
McLELLAND, Robert F.	Private	Private	The Cameronians (Scottish Rifles)	—	—	—
McLELLAND, Thomas A.	2nd Lieutenant	2nd Lieutenant	Argyll & Sutherland Highlanders	—	—	—
MACLENNAN, Alastair Grant	Private	Captain	14th London Regiment (London Scottish)	—	Mentioned in Despatches twice Military Cross Italian War Cross	France, 1916–1917 Italy, 1917–1918
MACLENNAN, Hamish Graeme	Private	Lieutenant	Royal Army Service Corps	Invalided, November 1918	—	France, 1914–1918
MACLENNAN, Ian M.	2nd Lieutenant	Captain	9th Battn. The Royal Scots (Royal Regiment)	Wounded, April 1917	Military Cross	France and Belgium, 1915–1917
✠ McLEOD, Alexander	Sub-Lieutenant	Sub-Lieutenant	Collingwood Battn. Royal Naval Division	Killed in action, 4th June, 1915, at Cape Helles	—	Gallipoli, 1915
MACLEOD, Donald	Chaplain 4th Class	Chaplain 3rd Class	Royal Army Chaplains Department	—	Mentioned in Despatches twice Military Cross	France and Belgium, 1916–1918

NAME.	RANK. At beginning of War or on joining.	RANK. At end of War.	UNIT.	CASUALTIES.	HONOURS OR DECORATIONS.	FIELD OF SERVICE.
MacLeod, Eric Louis Hay	Private	2nd Lieutenant	28th (County of London) Battn. The London Regiment (Artists Rifles) Royal Air Force	Wounded	—	—
✠ MacLeod, George Calder	2nd Lieutenant	Lieutenant	9th Battn. King's Own Scottish Borderers	Killed in action, 19th April, 1917, at Gaza	—	Gallipoli, 1915 Egypt and Palestine, 1916–1917
MacLeod, John Norman, M.B.	Lieut-Colonel	Lieut-Colonel	Indian Medical Service	—	—	—
MacLeod, John Norman Hay	Private	Private	Lowland Division Cyclist Corps Highland Light Infantry	Wounded	—	—
MacLeod, Norman	Captain	Lieut.-Colonel	Queen's Own Cameron Highlanders	Wounded, September 1915 Gassed, July 1918	Mentioned in Despatches three times Companion of the Order of St. Michael and St. George Distinguished Service Order Officer of the Legion of Honour	France, 1915–1918
McLeod, Norman	Private	Captain and Flight Commander	9th (G.H.) Battn. Highland Light Infantry Royal Flying Corps Royal Air Force	—	—	France, 1914–1917

NAME.	RANK. At beginning of War or on joining.	RANK. At end of War.	UNIT.	CASUALTIES.	HONOURS OR DECORATIONS.	FIELD OF SERVICE.
MACLEOD, Robert Lockhart Ross	Lieut.-Colonel	Colonel	Royal Army Medical Corps	—	Mentioned in Despatches four times Companion of the Order of the Bath Commander of the Order of the British Empire	France and Belgium, 1914–1918
McLEOD, William Hector	2nd Lieutenant	Lieutenant	7th Battn. Highland Light Infantry	Invalided, May 1917	—	France, 1916–1917
McMICHAEL, James	2nd Lieutenant	Lieutenant	9th (G.H.) Battn. The Highland Light Infantry	—	Mentioned in Despatches Military Cross	—
MACMILLAN, Donald Douglas	Private	Lieutenant	17th Battn. Highland Light Infantry The Cameronians (Scottish Rifles)	Wounded, September 1915 Invalided, May 1916 Wounded, April 1917 Wounded, April 1918	Military Cross	France, 1915–1918
MACMILLAN, John	2nd Lieutenant	Major	The Cameronians (Scottish Rifles)	Wounded, April 1916	Military Cross Bar to Military Cross	Gallipoli, 1915 Egypt, 1916 Mesopotamia, 1916–1918
✠ MACMILLAN, Thomas	Private	2nd Lieutenant	2nd Battn. Queen's Own Cameron Highlanders Royal Flying Corps	Wounded and gassed, 22nd/30th April, 1915 Accidentally killed, 12th March, 1917	—	France, 1915 Greece, 1915–1916
MacNABB, Hugh	Cadet	Captain	Inns of Court Officers Training Corps Lovat's Scouts	—	—	India, 1917–1918

Name.	Rank. At beginning of War or on joining.	Rank. At end of War.	Unit.	Casualties.	Honours or Decorations.	Field of Service.
MacNaughtan, A. G.	Lieutenant	Captain	9th (G.H.) Battn. Highland Light Infantry	—	—	—
MacNaughtan Charles John	Lieutenant	Lieutenant	9th (G.H.) Battn. Highland Light Infantry	Wounded, July 1916	—	France, 1916
McNeill, Ian Douglas	2nd Lieutenant	2nd Lieutenant	Highland Light Infantry	Prisoner of War	—	—
✠ McNeill, Nigel Lorne	2nd Lieutenant	2nd Lieutenant	Gordon Highlanders	Killed in action, 1st July, 1916	—	France
✠ McNicol, James Percival	2nd Lieutenant	Lieutenant	Argyll & Sutherland Highlanders	Died of wounds, 20th June, 1918	—	France, 1918
Macphail, Ronald M.	Orderly	2nd Lieutenant	Young Men's Christian Association; Glasgow University Officers Training Corps; Argyll & Sutherland Highlanders	Wounded, 1918	—	France
Macpherson, Ian	Cadet	Lieutenant	Glasgow University Officers Training Corps; The Rifle Brigade	Wounded, December 1917	—	France, 1917
McPherson, James Loran	Trooper	Lieutenant	3rd Scottish Horse; 6th Battn. Highland Light Infantry; Royal Air Force	Invalided, 1917; Wounded, 1918	—	Salonika, 1916; France, 1918

NAME.	RANK. At beginning of War or on joining.	RANK. At end of War.	UNIT.	CASUALTIES.	HONOURS OR DECORATIONS.	FIELD OF SERVICE.
MACQUAKER, Harry Morton	Trooper	Cadet	Queen's Own Royal Glasgow Yeomanry	Invalided, November 1917 and September 1918	—	France, 1915–1918
MACQUAKER, Thomas Mason	2nd Lieutenant	Captain	6th Battn. Highland Light Infantry	Invalided, November 1915	Military Cross	Gallipoli, 1915 Egypt and Palestine, 1916–1918
McVEAN, Alex. H. G.	Private	Private	39th Battn. Canadian Infantry	Wounded, April 1918	—	France
McVEAN, Donald Archibald Dugald, D.S.O.	Major	Colonel	45th Rattray's Sikhs, (Indian Army)	—	Mentioned in Despatches three times Bar to Distinguished Service Order Companion of the Order of the Star of India	Iraq, 1917–1918
McWATTERS, Robert William	Orderly	Lieutenant	Red Cross Service Gordon Highlanders	Wounded, April 1917 Invalided, June 1917	—	France, 1917
MADDEN, Henry Earle	Lance-Corporal	Corporal	Highland Light Infantry			—
✠ MAIN, George Ernest	2nd Lieutenant	Lieutenant	King's Own Scottish Borderers	Killed in action, 12th October, 1917	Mentioned in Despatches	France
✠ MAIN, Halcro Drummond	Private	Sergeant	Australian Infantry	Died of wounds received in action, 12th April, 1917, on the Somme	Military Medal	Egypt, 1915 Gallipoli, 1916 France, 1916–1917
MAIN, John William	2nd Lieutenant	Captain	5th Battn. Highland Light Infantry	Invalided, October 1915 Invalided, September 1917 Wounded, November 1917	—	Gallipoli, 1915 Egypt, 1916–1917 France, 1918

NAME.	RANK. At beginning of War or on joining.	RANK. At end of War.	UNIT.	CASUALTIES.	HONOURS OR DECORATIONS.	FIELD OF SERVICE.
MAIN, Peter Clark	Engineer Sub-Lieutenant	Engineer Lieutenant	Royal Naval Reserve	—	—	At Sea, 1915–1918
MAIR, Arthur M.	Private	Lieutenant	7th Battn. Royal Scots Fusiliers	Invalided, September 1916	—	France, 1915–1916 and 1918
MAIR, Frederick Clark	Gunner	Flight Lieutenant	Royal Field Artillery; 7th Battn. Highland Light Infantry; Royal Flying Corps	Invalided, October 1915	Mentioned in Despatches	Gallipoli, 1915; Egypt, Palestine, Mesopotamia, India, 1916–1918
MAIR, William	2nd Lieutenant	Captain	7th Battn. Highland Light Infantry	—	—	Egypt, 1916–1918; France, 1918
✠ MALCOLM, Archibald Houlder	2nd Lieutenant	Lieutenant	9th (G.H.) Battn. Highland Light Infantry	Wounded, August 1916; Killed in action, 24th August, 1918	—	France, 1916; Egypt, 1918; France, 1918
✠ MALCOLM, James Waddell	2nd Lieutenant	2nd Lieutenant	5th Battn. Highland Light Infantry	Killed in action, 12th July, 1915, at Cape Helles	Mentioned in Despatches	Gallipoli, 1915
✠ MARR, James S.	Private	Captain	17th Battn. Highland Light Infantry	Killed in action, 18th November, 1916	—	France, 1915–1916
MARR, William H.	Trooper	Trooper	Calcutta Light Horse	—	—	—
✠ MARSHALL, Alexander Balfour	2nd Lieutenant	2nd Lieutenant	3rd Battn. The Cameronians (Scottish Rifles)	Killed in action, 7th December, 1915	—	Suvla Bay and Dorian Front, 1915

G

Name.	Rank. At beginning of War or on joining.	Rank. At end of War.	Unit.	Casualties.	Honours or Decorations.	Field of Service.
✠ MARSHALL, Bertram	Private	Sergeant	Canadian Forces	Killed in action, 24th August, 1918	—	France
MARSHALL, George	2nd Lieutenant	Major	Royal Army Medical Corps	—	Mentioned in Despatches twice	France, 1918
✠ MARSHALL, Hubert G. H.	Private	2nd Lieutenant	Royal Army Medical Corps / Royal Tank Corps	Missing, August/September, found killed in Tank, 2nd September, 1918	—	France, 1918
MARSHALL, Robert Macnab	Lieutenant	Captain	Royal Army Medical Corps	Invalided, December 1918	—	France, 1916-1918
MARTIN, Alexander Elsden	Despatch Rider	Lieutenant	Royal Engineers	—	—	France, 1914-1918
MARTIN, Douglas M.	Private	Lieutenant	9th (G.H.) Battn. Highland Light Infantry / Gordon Highlanders / Royal Air Force	—	—	France, 1916-1917
MARTIN, Fred Robertson	Private	Private	Royal Army Medical Corps	—	—	—
MARTIN, Harold E. L.	Private	Lieutenant	Royal Engineers	—	Mentioned in Despatches	Mediterranean Expeditionary Force, 1915-1916 / Mesopotamia, 1917-1918
MARTIN, James	2nd Lieutenant	Lieutenant	8th Battn. Highland Light Infantry	Wounded	Mentioned in Despatches / Military Cross	France

Name.	Rank. At beginning of War or on joining.	Rank. At end of War.	Unit.	Casualties.	Honours or Decorations.	Field of Service.
Martin, William Foulds Junr.	Private	Lieutenant	Argyll & Sutherland Highlanders	—	—	France, 1916; Africa, 1917–1918
Martin, William Marshall	2nd Lieutenant	2nd Lieutenant	The Black Watch (Royal Highlanders)	—	—	—
Mason, George J.	Bombardier	Bombardier	Royal Field Artillery	—	—	France, 1917; Italy, 1917–1918
Mason, William Linn	2nd Lieutenant	Captain	Royal Army Service Corps	Invalided, November 1915 January 1916 and December 1917–February 1918	Mentioned in Despatches twice; Order of the Nile, 4th Class	Gallipoli, 1915; Salonika, 1916–1917; Palestine, 1917–1918
Mavor, Eric Ingram	2nd Lieutenant	2nd Lieutenant	6th Battn. Highland Light Infantry	Wounded, July 1915 Discharged, September 1916	—	Gallipoli, 1915
Mavor, John Bridie	Lieutenant	Major	Royal Engineers	Invalided, 1917	—	Home Service
Mavor, Osborne Henry	Lieutenant	Major	Royal Army Medical Corps	Invalided, February 1917	Mentioned in Despatches	Belgium, 1915–1916; France, 1916–1917; Mesopotamia, 1917–1918; N. Persia and S. Russia, 1918
Meadus, Reginald Harold	Gunner	Gunner	Royal Canadian Horse Artillery	Invalided, August 1917 Invalided, August 1918	—	Belgium and France, 1915

Name.	Rank. At beginning of War or on joining.	Rank. At end of War.	Unit.	Casualties.	Honours or Decorations.	Field of Service.
✠ MECHAN, Arthur Clifford	Private	Corporal	Queen's Own Cameron Highlanders	Killed in action, 25/27th September, 1915, at Loos	—	France, 1915
MEGLAUGHLIN, Denis S.	Lieutenant	Captain	Red Cross Motor Transport	—	—	Home Service
MEIKLE, William, Junr.	Major	Lieut.-Colonel	6th Battn. Highland Light Infantry	—	Mentioned in Despatches three times	Home Service
MELVILLE, Patrick Stewart	Private	2nd Lieutenant	5th Battn. Cameron Highlanders	Wounded, September 1916	Military Cross	France, 1915–1916 and 1917–1918
MELVIN, Kenneth T.	Private	Private	5th Battn. The Cameronians (Scottish Rifles)	—	—	—
MICHIE, Arthur Smith	Sergeant	Sergeant	1st Battn. The Hertfordshire Regiment	Invalided, March 1917	—	India, 1916–1917
MICHIE, Charles E.	Lance-Corporal	Lance-Corporal	24th Battn. The Rifle Brigade	Invalided, May 1917	—	India, 1916–1917
MICHIE, Robert Andrew	Private	Paymaster Lieutenant	1st Battn. The Cambridgeshire Regiment Royal Naval Volunteer Reserve	Discharged, August 1916	—	Home Service
✠ MILL, James Davidson	Private	Private	6th Battn. Queen's Own Cameron Highlanders	Killed in action, 26th September, 1915, at Loos	—	France, 1915
✠ MILL, William Randall Clunas	Private	Private	Royal Army Medical Corps	Killed in action, 27th May, 1918	—	Gallipoli, 1915 Egypt, 1916–1917 Palestine, 1917–1918 France, 1918

Name.	Rank. At beginning of War or on joining.	Rank. At end of War.	Unit.	Casualties.	Honours or Decorations.	Field of Service.
MILLAR, Arthur Scoular	2nd Lieutenant	Captain	17th Battn. Highland Light Infantry	Wounded, July 1916	—	France, 1915-1916 Persia, 1918
MILLAR, Brian Reynolds	Flight Sub-Lieutenant	Captain	Royal Naval Air Service	—	—	North Sea and English Channel, 1917-1918
MILLAR, Frederick James Steel	Private	Captain	9th (G.H.) Battn. Highland Light Infantry 9th Battn. The Cameronians (Scottish Rifles)	Wounded	Military Cross Bar to Military Cross	France, 1914-1918
✠ MILLAR, James Ainslie	Private	2nd Lieutenant	17th Battn. Highland Light Infantry Royal Scots Fusiliers	Reported missing, after attack on 25th September, 1915, at Sanctuary Wood	—	France, 1915
MILLER, Alan Wingate	Lieutenant	Lieutenant	Royal Engineers Attached Royal Flying Corps	Wounded and Prisoner of War, April 1918	—	France, 1916-1918
MILLER, Alexander Wilson	2nd Lieutenant	2nd Lieutenant	Royal Engineers	—	—	—
MILLER, Archibald Elliot Haswell	2nd Lieutenant	Lieutenant	7th (Blythswood) Battn. Highland Light Infantry	Wounded, August 1918	Military Cross	Palestine, 1917 France, 1918
MILLER, Charles D.	Private	Captain	Argyll & Sutherland Highlanders	—	—	France and Belgium, 1918
MILLER, Hugh	Captain	Captain	Royal Army Medical Corps	—	—	—

NAME.	RANK. At beginning of War or on joining.	RANK. At end of War.	UNIT.	CASUALTIES.	HONOURS OR DECORATIONS.	FIELD OF SERVICE.
MILLER, James S.	Private	Private	The Royal Scots (Royal Regiment)	—	—	—
✠ MILLER, Kenneth Steven	Private	Lieutenant	17th Battn. Highland Light Infantry. The Cameronians (Scottish Rifles) 4th Battn.	Wounded, July 1916. Wounded and missing—presumed killed, 1st August, 1917	—	France, 1915–1917
MILLER, Robert Monteith	Lieutenant	Captain	5th Battn. Highland Light Infantry	Invalided, August 1915. Wounded and Prisoner of War, August 1918	—	Gallipoli, 1915. Palestine, 1917. France, 1918
MILLIGAN, John Whiteford Cumming	Cadet	Cadet	Edinburgh University Officers Training Corps	—	—	—
MILLIGAN, William Reid	Lance-Corporal	Lieutenant	The Cameronians (Scottish Rifles)	—	—	—
MILNE, William M.	Driver	Driver	British Red Cross Motor Section	—	—	France, 1916–1917
MITCHELL, Alexander D. S.	Captain	Captain	Argyll & Sutherland Highlanders	Wounded	—	—
MITCHELL, C. Harold	Gunner	Gunner	Royal Field Artillery	—	—	—
MITCHELL, John B. C. Cameron	Lieutenant	Captain	Royal Engineers	—	Military Cross	Belgium and France, 1915–1918

NAME.	RANK. At beginning of War or on joining.	RANK. At end of War.	UNIT.	CASUALTIES.	HONOURS OR DECORATIONS.	FIELD OF SERVICE.
MITCHELL, Robert E.	Private	Captain	5th Battn. The Cameronians (Scottish Rifles)	Wounded, July 1916 Wounded, May 1918	—	France, 1915–1916 and 1913
MITCHELL, Thomas Greenwood	2nd Lieutenant	Lieutenant	Royal Engineers	—	Mentioned in Despatches	France, 1917–1918
MITCHELL, William Baxter	2nd Lieutenant	Lieutenant	Royal Engineers	—	—	France and Belgium, 1918
MONTGOMERY, Daniel	Private	2nd Lieutenant	The Cameronians (Scottish Rifles) Highland Light Infantry	—	—	—
MONTGOMERY, George Allison	Private	Lieutenant	5th Battn. Highland Light Infantry	—	—	Home Service
✠ MONTEITH, William Albert Robertson	2nd Lieutenant	2nd Lieutenant	2nd Battn. Seaforth Highlanders	Died of wounds, 2nd September, 1918, at Arras	—	France
✠ MORISON, W. Donald	Private	Lance-Corporal	6th Battn. King's Own Scottish Borderers	Killed in action, 25th September, 1915, at Loos	—	France, 1915
✠ MORRISON, Alexander W.	Private	Private	Gordon Highlanders	Killed in action, 1918	—	France, 1918
MORRISON, Arthur Russell Inglis	Cadet	Cadet	Glasgow University Officers Training Corps	—	—	Home Service

Name.	Rank. At beginning of War or on joining.	Rank. At end of War.	Unit.	Casualties.	Honours or Decorations.	Field of Service.
✠ MORRISON, Arthur Stanley	2nd Lieutenant	Lieutenant	Royal Garrison Artillery	Killed in action, 23rd August, 1918, near Arras	—	France, 1918
✠ MORRISON, James Ian	2nd Lieutenant	2nd Lieutenant	Royal Scots Fusiliers	Killed in action	—	France
MORRISON, Leslie S.	Cadet Sergeant	2nd Lieutenant	Glasgow University Officers Training Corps No. 11 Officer Cadet Battn. 5th Battn. Highland Light Infantry	—	—	Home Service
MORRISON, Ronald Harvey	Lieutenant	Captain	5th Battn. Highland Light Infantry	—	Mentioned in Despatches Military Cross Bar to Military Cross	Gallipoli, 1915 Egypt and Palestine, 1916–1918 France, 1918
MORTON, John W.	Private	2nd Lieutenant	Royal Army Medical Corps Highland Light Infantry	—	—	—
MORTON, Robert Corson	Lance-Corporal	Lance-Corporal	Highland Light Infantry	—	—	—
MORTON, Robert	Cadet	Cadet	Edinburgh University Officers Training Corps	—	—	Home Service
✠ MOTHERWELL, William	2nd Lieutenant	2nd Lieutenant	Highland Light Infantry Royal Engineers	Killed in action, 5th March, 1917	—	France

NAME.	RANK. At beginning of War or on joining.	RANK. At end of War.	UNIT.	CASUALTIES.	HONOURS OR DECORATIONS.	FIELD OF SERVICE.
MOTHERWELL, William	Lieutenant	Captain	Royal Engineers	Invalided	—	—
✠ MOWAT, Charles James Carlton	Lieutenant	Captain	8th Battn. The Cameronians (Scottish Rifles)	Killed in action, 28th June, 1915, at Cape Helles	—	Gallipoli, 1915
MOWAT, D. Gordon	Private	Private	Gordon Highlanders	—	—	—
MOWAT, John, M.B.	Lieutenant	Captain	Royal Army Medical Corps		—	—
MUIR, Alan MacDonald	Private	Lieutenant	Argyll & Sutherland Highlanders	—	—	Home Service
✠ MUIR, Alexander	Private	2nd Lieutenant	9th (G.H.) Battn. Highland Light Infantry; 6th Battn. Highland Light Infantry	Wounded, May 1915; Died of wounds, 27th July, 1916	—	France, 1914–1916
MUIR, James	Lieutenant	Lieutenant	Rangoon Mounted Rifles	—	—	Burma, 1914–1918
MUIR, Morris C.	Lieutenant	Major	5th Battn. Queen's Own Cameron Highlanders	Wounded, April 1917; Wounded, March 1918; Wounded, July 1918	Military Cross	France, 1915–1918
MUIR, Robert	Private	Private	Royal Army Service Corps	—	—	—
MUIR, Stanley R. C.	Lance-Corporal	Lieutenant	Argyll & Sutherland Highlanders; West African Frontier Force	—	—	France, 1916; Gold Coast, West Africa, 1918

Name.	Rank. At beginning of War or on joining.	Rank. At end of War.	Unit.	Casualties.	Honours or Decorations.	Field of Service.
MUIRHEAD, George Paterson	Cadet	2nd Lieutenant	Officer Cadet Battn. Argyll & Sutherland Highlanders	—	—	—
✠ MUNRO, James N.	Private	Private	South African Infantry	Killed in action, 20th September, 1917	—	France
MURDOCH, Alexander Oliver	Sergeant	Staff Sergeant	Royal Army Service Corps	—	—	Home Service
MURDOCH, Eric G.	Corporal	Lieutenant	Royal Field Artillery	Wounded	—	—
MURDOCH, James Cameron	Sub-Lieutenant	Lieutenant	Royal Naval Volunteer Reserve	—	—	North Sea, 1915–1918
MURDOCH, Rudolf T. G.	Private	Private	Shanghai Volunteers	—	—	—
MURDOCH, Vivian Falconer	Cadet	2nd Lieutenant	Officer Cadet Battalion Gordon Highlanders	Wounded	Military Cross	France, 1917–1918
✠ MURRAY, Alexander Roxburgh	2nd Lieutenant	2nd Lieutenant	17th Battn. Highland Light Infantry	Killed in action, 18th November, 1916, at Beaumont-Hamel	—	France, 1916
✠ MURRAY, Andrew Currie	2nd Lieutenant	Captain	1st Battn. Highland Light Infantry Attached 9th (G.H.) Battn. Highland Light Infantry	Wounded, May 1915; Killed in action, 20th May, 1917, at Bullecoeur, South of Arras	—	France, 1914–1917

NAME.	RANK. At beginning of War or on joining.	RANK. At end of War.	UNIT.	CASUALTIES.	HONOURS OR DECORATIONS.	FIELD OF SERVICE.
MURRAY, Archibald W.	Private	Captain	17th Battn. Highland Light Infantry 8th Battn. Royal Scots Fusiliers 7th Battn. King's Own Scottish Borderers Machine Gun Corps	Wounded, July 1916	—	France and Belgium, 1915–1918
MURRAY, Arthur Goudie	Flight Cadet	Flight Cadet	Royal Air Force	—	—	Home Service
MURRAY, Charles de Bois	Private	2nd Lieutenant	Highland Light Infantry Royal Scots Fusiliers King's Own Scottish Borderers	—	—	—
MURRAY, George M.	Cadet	Cadet	Glasgow University Officers Training Corps	—	—	Home Service
MURRAY, Ian	2nd Lieutenant	2nd Lieutenant	Labour Corps	—	—	Home Service
MURRAY, J. A.	Lieutenant	Captain	Royal Army Medical Corps	—	—	—
MURRAY, James Campbell	2nd Lieutenant	Lieutenant	10th Battn. The Black Watch (Royal Highlanders)	Invalided, May 1916	—	France, 1915–1916 East Africa and Somaliland 1918
MURRAY, L. D.	Captain	Major	7th Battn. The Highland Light Infantry	—	—	—

Name.	Rank. At beginning of War or on joining.	Rank. At end of War.	Unit.	Casualties.	Honours or Decorations.	Field of Service.
✠ Murray, Randolph	2nd Lieutenant	Lieutenant	Queen's Own Cameron Highlanders	Twice invalided. Died of wounds received in action, 27th October, 1917	—	France, 1916–1917
✠ Murray, Ronald Alexander	2nd Lieutenant	Captain	8th Battn. Royal Scots Fusiliers	Killed in action, 19th September, 1918	—	France, 1915. Salonica, 1918
Murray, Thomas Burns Jeffrey	2nd Lieutenant	2nd Lieutenant	Royal Tank Corps	—	—	Home Service
Nance, William J. de	Private	Private	Royal Army Medical Corps	—	—	—
Napier, Frederick Lewis	Lieutenant	Captain	Royal Army Medical Corps	Injured, February 1916	Mentioned in Despatches	France, 1914–1918
Neilson, J. B.	Private	Private	14th London Regiment (London Scottish)	—	—	—
Nelson, Donald R.	2nd Lieutenant	Major	7th Battn. The Cameronians (Scottish Rifles)	Invalided, November 1915. Wounded, August 1917. Wounded, December 1917	Mentioned in Despatches. Military Cross	Gallipoli, 1915. Palestine, 1916–1918. France and Belgium, 1918
✠ Nelson, Graham	2nd Lieutenant	Lieutenant	The Cameronians (Scottish Rifles). Royal Flying Corps	Killed on Service, 30th August, 1917	—	France
✠ Nelson, J. Noel	2nd Lieutenant	Lieutenant	Royal Air Force	Killed in action, 18th June, 1918	—	France

Name.	Rank. At beginning of War or on joining.	Rank. At end of War.	Unit.	Casualties.	Honours or Decorations.	Field of Service.
Nelson, John Ewing	2nd Lieutenant	Lieutenant	The Cameronians (Scottish Rifles)	Invalided	—	—
Nelson, William Kenneth	Able Seaman	Able Seaman	Royal Naval Volunteer Reserve	Discharged, 'Under Age,' November 1917	—	Home Service
Newton, Stanley Duncan	Private	Lieutenant	9th (G.H.) Battn. Highland Light Infantry	Invalided, April 1915 Invalided, July 1919	—	France and Belgium, 1914-1915 East Africa, 1918
Nicholson, Clark	Lieutenant	Major	Royal Army Medical Corps	—	Mentioned in Despatches Military Cross Bar to Military Cross	France, 1915-1918
Nicol, Arthur M.	2nd Lieutenant	2nd Lieutenant	Royal Army Service Corps	—	—	—
✠ Nicol, David	2nd Lieutenant	Captain	Argyll & Sutherland Highlanders	Killed in action, 26th November, 1917, at Cambrai	—	France
Nicol, J. H.	Major	Major	Royal Army Medical Corps	—	—	Home Service
Nicol, Robert G.	Private	Lieutenant	The Cameronians (Scottish Rifles)	Wounded, October 1918	Military Cross	France, 1917-1918
Nicolson, Kenneth J.	2nd Lieutenant	Captain	Royal Artillery	Wounded, 1916	Mentioned in Despatches Military Cross	France and Belgium, 1916-1918

NAME.	RANK.		UNIT.	CASUALTIES.	HONOURS OR DECORATIONS.	FIELD OF SERVICE.
	At beginning of War or on joining.	At end of War.				
✠ NIMMO, James Ronald	Private	2nd Lieutenant	Scottish Horse The Cameronians (Scottish Rifles)	Killed by accident, 1st May, 1917, at Devonport	—	Gallipoli, 1915 Egypt, 1916
NIMMO, John Alan	2nd Lieutenant	Lieutenant	Royal Garrison Artillery	—	Mentioned in Despatches	Malta, 1914–1916 Egypt, 1916 Salonika, 1916–1918
NIVEN, Robert Ogilvie	2nd Lieutenant	Captain	Royal Engineers	—	—	France and Belgium, 1917–1918
NIVEN, T. Murray	Cadet	Cadet	Glasgow University Officers Training Corps	—	—	Home Service
NOTT, Louis P.	Major	Major	Royal Engineers	—	—	—
OGG, Archibald Craig Alexander	Private	Private	14th London Regiment (London Scottish)	Wounded, October 1916	—	France, 1916
OGG, George J., Junr.	Private	Lieutenant	9th (G.H.) Battn. Highland Light Infantry Royal Air Force	—	—	France, 1914–1917
OGG, Robert Allan	Lieutenant	Lieutenant	6th Battn. Highland Light Infantry	Wounded, September 1918	—	France, 1918
✠ OGG, William Kelly Carmichael	Private	2nd Lieutenant	9th (G.H.) Battn. Highland Light Infantry	Wounded and missing, 15th July, 1916	—	France, 1916
OLIPHANT, Alexander M.	Private	Lieutenant	Argyll & Sutherland Highlanders	Invalided, April 1917	—	France, 1917

Name.	Rank. At beginning of War or on joining.	Rank. At end of War.	Unit.	Casualties.	Honours or Decorations.	Field of Service.
ORMSBY, John Y.	Gentleman Cadet	Gentleman Cadet	Royal Military College, Sandhurst	—	—	Home Service
ORR, David Roy	Private	Major	11th Battn. The Cameronians (Scottish Rifles)	Wounded, September 1918	Mentioned in Despatches twice Military Cross	France, 1915 Salonika, 1915 Bulgaria, 1918
ORR, Frank George	Lieutenant	Lieut.-Colonel	Royal Field Artillery	Invalided, August 1915	Mentioned in Despatches twice Commander of the Order of the British Empire	Gallipoli, 1915
ORR, Henry Ross	2nd Lieutenant	Captain	17th Battn. Highland Light Infantry	Invalided, 1917	—	France, 1916-1917
ORR, Ian Morison	Cadet	Corporal	Glasgow University Officers Training Corps	—	—	Home Service
✠ ORR, Robert Baird Rowley	Private	Captain	9th (G.H.) Battn. Highland Light Infantry 9th Battn. Argyll & Sutherland Highlanders Royal Flying Corps	Gassed, 24th May, 1915 Killed while flying, 3rd July, 1917, on Ypres Salient	—	France, 1915-1917
✠ ORR, Robert Watson	2nd Lieutenant	2nd Lieutenant	18th The London Regiment (London Irish Rifles)	Killed in action, 25th September, 1915, at Loos	—	France, 1915
OSBORNE, Alexander Frank	Trooper	Trooper	Southern Provinces Mounted Rifles	—	—	India, 1914-1918

NAME.	RANK. At beginning of War or on joining.	RANK. At end of War.	UNIT.	CASUALTIES.	HONOURS OR DECORATIONS.	FIELD OF SERVICE.
OSBORNE, D. Wallace	Trooper	Trooper	Southern Provinces Mounted Rifles	—	—	India, 1914–1918
✠ OSBORNE, George Edward Bell	Captain	Major	Fife & Forfar Yeomanry	Killed in action, 6th November, 1917	—	—
OSBORNE, R. Thornton	Captain	Major	Canadian Field Artillery	—	Military Cross	France, 1915–1918
PAINE, James William Reginald	Private	Captain	6th Battn. Argyll & Sutherland Highlanders	—	—	France 1916–1917 and 1918 Italy, 1917–1918
PAISLEY, Peter	Lieutenant	Captain	Royal Tank Corps	Invalided, January 1919	Mentioned in Despatches	France, 1916–1917
PAISLEY, William Walker	Midshipman	Midshipman	Royal Naval Volunteer Reserve	—	—	At Sea, 1918
PARK, John Brown	2nd Lieutenant	Captain	5th Battn. The Cameronians (Scottish Rifles) 6th Battn. Queen's Own Cameron Highlanders	Wounded, 1918	Military Cross	France, 1916–1918
PARK, William Vass	Lieutenant	Lieutenant	5th Battn. The Cameronians (Scottish Rifles)	Wounded, November 1918	—	France, 1916–1918
PATE, Robert Thomas Alexander Affleck	Private	Captain	9th (G.H.) Battn. The Highland Light Infantry	Wounded, 1916	—	France, 1915–1918

THE ROLL OF THE FALLEN

Name.	Rank. At beginning of War or on joining.	Rank. At end of War.	Unit.	Casualties.	Honours or Decorations.	Field of Service.
PATE, Thomas Williamson	Private	Flight Cadet	Royal Army Service Corps Royal Flying Corps	—	—	Home Service
✠ PATERSON, Douglas William	2nd Lieutenant	2nd Lieutenant	The Border Regiment	Killed in action, 30th March, 1918	—	Flanders, 1917-1918
PATERSON, G. Kirk	Private	Captain	Highland Light Infantry Argyll & Sutherland Highlanders	—	—	—
PATERSON, Grahame F.	Private	Captain	5th Battn. The Black Watch (Royal Highlanders)	—	Mentioned in Despatches	France and Belgium 1916-1918
✠ PATERSON, Isla Scott	2nd Lieutenant	Captain	5th Battn. The Black Watch (Royal Highlanders)	Wounded, 14th October, 1916 Killed in action, 1st November, 1917	Military Cross	France, 1915-1917
PATERSON, James	Gunner	Gunner	Gossipore Artillery Volunteers	—	—	—
PATERSON, William Gavin	2nd Lieutenant	Captain	The Cameronians (Scottish Rifles)	Wounded, October 1916	—	France and Belgium, 1916
✠ PATERSON, William Wilson	Private	2nd Lieutenant	9th (G.H.) Battn. Highland Light Infantry	Killed in action, 15th July, 1916, on the Somme	—	France, 1914-1916
PATON, Archibald M.	Lieutenant	Lieutenant	Royal Naval Volunteer Reserve	—	—	Home Service

H

NAME.	RANK. At beginning of War or on joining.	RANK. At end of War.	UNIT.	CASUALTIES.	HONOURS OR DECORATIONS.	FIELD OF SERVICE.
PATON, George C.	1st Class Air Mechanic	1st Class Air Mechanic	Royal Flying Corps	—	—	France and Belgium, 1916–1918
PATON, J.	Lieutenant	Lieutenant	Argyll & Sutherland Highlanders	—	—	—
PATON, Richard R. K.	Lieutenant	Captain	Royal Army Medical Corps	—	Mentioned in Despatches twice	France, 1914 and 1917–1918
PATON, Robert A. R.	Trooper	Trooper	South African Heavy Artillery	—	—	—
PATON, William Alexander	Despatch Rider	Corporal	Royal Engineers	—	—	France, 1914–1918
PATON, William Calder	Lieutenant	Major	Indian Medical Service	Invalided, September 1915	Mentioned in Despatches twice Military Cross Brevet Major	France, 1914–1915 Mesopotamia, 1916–1918 Palestine, 1918
PATON, William M.	Trooper	Trooper	Queen's Own Royal Glasgow Yeomanry	—	—	—
PATTERSON, J. C.	Private	Private	Royal Army Service Corps	—	—	—
PATTERSON, John Turner	2nd Lieutenant	2nd Lieutenant	Highland Light Infantry	—	—	—
PATTERSON, Robert Wilson	2nd Lieutenant	Captain	Royal Engineers Royal Flying Corps Royal Air Force	Invalided	—	France and Belgium, 1915–1916

NAME.	RANK. At beginning of War or on joining.	RANK. At end of War.	UNIT.	CASUALTIES.	HONOURS OR DECORATIONS.	FIELD OF SERVICE.
PATTISON, James William Henry	Lieutenant	Major	8th Battn. The Cameronians (Scottish Rifles)	Invalided, 1916 and 1917	Mentioned in Despatches	Gallipoli, 1915; Egypt, 1916–1917
✠ PATTISON, Robert Macfie	2nd Lieutenant	Lieutenant	8th Battn. The Cameronians (Scottish Rifles)	Reported missing, 28th June, 1915	—	Gallipoli, 1915
PAUL, George Alexander	Corporal	Corporal	Glasgow University Officers Training Corps	—	—	Home Service
PAUL, Harold D.	Cadet	Cadet	Glasgow University Officers Training Corps	—	—	Home Service
✠ PAUL, Robert MacLeod	Private	Private	17th Battn. Highland Light Infantry	Missing, 1st July, 1916	—	France, 1915–1916
PAUL, Robert S.	Major	Lieut-Colonel	Baluchistan Infantry (Indian Army)	—	—	—
PEACE, A. G.	Corporal	Corporal	Calcutta Scottish	—	—	—
PEAT, James M.	Cadet	Cadet	Edinburgh University Officers Training Corps	—	—	Home Service
PEAT, P. Sandeman W.	2nd Lieutenant	2nd Lieutenant	14th Battn. Northumberland Fusiliers	—	—	France, 1918
PEEBLES, Archibald	2nd Lieutenant	2nd Lieutenant	Madras & Southern Mahratta Railway Rifles	—	—	—
PEEBLES, Robert Eric	Lieutenant	Captain	Royal Field Artillery	Wounded	—	—

Name.	Rank. At beginning of War or on joining.	Rank. At end of War.	Unit.	Casualties.	Honours or Decorations.	Field of Service.
✠ PEEBLES, William Fleming	2nd Lieutenant	Lieutenant	The Border Regiment Machine Gun Corps	Killed in action, 30th April, 1917	—	France
PEOCK, William Donald	Cadet	Lieutenant	Royal Air Force	—	—	Home Service
✠ PERRY, Alexander Ernest	Private	Lance-Corporal	Queen's Own Cameron Highlanders	Killed in Action, 26th September, 1915, at Loos	—	France, 1915
PETERSEN, G. G. Wingaard	2nd Lieutenant	2nd Lieutenant	Royal Flying Corps	—	—	—
PETERSON, Oluf C. W.	Trooper	2nd Lieutenant	Queen's Own Royal Glasgow Yeomanry Highland Light Infantry	—	—	—
PETRIE, James	Private	Private	Royal Army Service Corps	—	—	France, 1916–1918
PHILLIPS, Alexander	Lieutenant	Lieutenant	9th (G.H.) Battn. Highland Light Infantry	Wounded, December 1916 Wounded, July 1918	Military Cross	France and Belgium, 1916 and 1918
PICKERING, J. Lynn K.	Sergeant	Sergeant	Australian Imperial Forces	Invalided, August 1917	—	France, 1915–1917
✠ PINNEY, Kingsley William Guy	Private	Cadet	The Suffolk Regiment No. 12 Officer Cadet Battn.	Died, 10th July, 1917, in Yorkhill War Hospital	—	Home Service
POOLEY, Francis Henry	Private	Captain	17th Battn. The Highland Light Infantry Tank Corps	Wounded twice	—	France, 1916–1918

NAME.	RANK. At beginning of War or on joining.	RANK. At end of War.	UNIT.	CASUALTIES.	HONOURS OR DECORATIONS.	FIELD OF SERVICE.
PORTEOUS, D. A.	Private	Private	Highland Light Infantry	—	—	—
PRATT, Arthur Alfred	Major	Major	Royal Army Medical Corps	—	—	—
✠ PRICE, Charles Thomas	Private	2nd Lieutenant	9th (G.H.) Battn. Highland Light Infantry 5th Battn. Highland Light Infantry	Killed in action, 30th November, 1917	—	Egypt, 1917
PURDIE, Clifford	2nd Lieutenant	2nd Lieutenant	The Cameronians (Scottish Rifles)	—	—	—
✠ PURDIE, Thomas Paterson	2nd Lieutenant	2nd Lieutenant	The Welch Regiment	Killed in action, 9th July, 1918	—	France
QUAILE, Kenneth McEwen	Lieutenant	Lieutenant	Argyll & Sutherland Highlanders	Invalided, March 1918	—	France, 1917-1918
RAE, Robert Muir	Private	Lieutenant	Scottish Horse	Wounded, May 1915 Prisoner of War, March 1918	—	Egypt, 1916 Salonika, 1916-1917 France, 1917-1918
RAE, W. Wallace	Cadet	Cadet	Royal Flying Corps School	—	—	Home Service
RALSTON, David	Lieutenant	Major	6th Battn. The Cameronians (Scottish Rifles) Machine-Gun Corps	Wounded, 1916	Mentioned in Despatches twice Military Cross Bar to Military Cross	France, 1915-1918

Name.	Rank. At beginning of War or on joining.	Rank. At end of War.	Unit.	Casualties.	Honours or Decorations.	Field of Service.
RALSTON, John Steel	2nd Lieutenant	Captain	8th Battn. The Cameronians (Scottish Rifles) Royal Flying Corps Royal Air Force	Wounded twice	Military Cross Distinguished Flying Cross	Egypt, 1916 France, 1917–1918
RAMSEY, Bryce Buchanan	2nd Lieutenant	Major	Royal Scots Fusiliers	Gassed, April 1918	Military Cross	France, 1915–1918
RANKIN, Henry Charles Deans	Lieutenant	Lieut.-Colonel	Royal Army Medical Corps	Prisoner of War, September 1914 and November 1917	Mentioned in Despatches three times Officer of the Order of the British Empire	France and Flanders, 1914–1918
✠ RANKIN, James Kerr Patrick	Private	Private	Highland Light Infantry	Killed in action 1st July, 1916	—	France
✠ RANKIN, James Thomson	2nd Lieutenant	2nd Lieutenant	4th Battn. Argyll & Sutherland Highlanders	Killed in action, 23rd December, 1915, at Gallipoli	—	Gallipoli, 1915
RANKINE, Adam	Lieutenant	Major	Royal Army Medical Corps	—	Mentioned in Despatches Military Cross	Mediterranean Expeditionary Force, 1915 Egypt, 1916–1918
RANKINE, David	Cadet	—	Glasgow University Officers Training Corps	—	—	Home Service
RANKINE, J. Graham	Private	Lieutenant	5th Battn. Queen's Own Cameron Highlanders	Invalided, May 1916 Invalided, August 1918	—	France, 1915–1916
RANKINE, Thomas G.	2nd Lieutenant	2nd Lieutenant	Lothian & Border Horse Royal Scots Fusiliers	—	—	East Africa, 1917–1918

NAME.	RANK. At beginning of War or on joining.	RANK. At end of War.	UNIT.	CASUALTIES.	HONOURS OR DECORATIONS.	FIELD OF SERVICE.
REID, Charles	Private	Sergeant	7th Battn. The Black Watch (Royal High-landers)	—	—	France and Belgium, 1918
REID, Douglas Neilson	2nd Lieu-tenant	Lieutenant	Highland Light Infantry	—	—	Egypt, 1917 Indian Frontier, 1917 Egypt, 1918
REID, Francis Warrack	Lieutenant	Captain	16th Battn. Highland Light Infantry	Wounded, July 1916	Military Cross	France, 1915–1918
REID, George Ure	Engine Room Artificer	Engine Room Artificer	Royal Navy	—	—	At Sea
REID, Gordon Cairns	Corporal Despatch Rider	Corporal Despatch Rider	Royal Engineers	—	—	France, 1917–1918
REID, James Macarthur	Cadet	Cadet	Glasgow University Offi-cers Training Corps	—	—	Home Service
REID, W. Cecil	2nd Lieu-tenant	2nd Lieu-tenant	Royal Engineers	—	—	Home Service
REIS, Eric M. W.	Private	Lance-Corporal	9th (G.H.) Battn. High-land Light Infantry	Invalided, 1914	—	France, 1914–1918
REITH, (Rev.) Archibald, M.A.	Chaplain	Chaplain	Army Chaplains Depart-ment	—	—	—
REITH, George Douglas	Chaplain	Chaplain	Young Men's Christian Association	—	—	France, 1914–1915 and 1918

NAME.	RANK. At beginning of War or on joining.	RANK. At end of War.	UNIT.	CASUALTIES.	HONOURS OR DECORATIONS.	FIELD OF SERVICE.
REITH, John Charles Walsham	Lieutenant	Major	5th Battn. The Cameronians (Scottish Rifles) Royal Engineers	Wounded, October 1915	—	France, 1914–1915 United States of America, 1916–1917
RENNIE, Andrew Gerald	Lieutenant	Captain	Royal Army Service Corps	—	—	—
RENNIE, Hugh Wylie	2nd Lieutenant	Captain	Argyll & Sutherland Highlanders	Invalided, November 1916	—	France, 1915 Salonika, 1915–1916
RENNIE, John D.	Major	Major	Royal Air Force	—	—	Home Service
✠ RENNIE, Malcolm Stark	Private	Private	5th Battn. Seaforth Highlanders	Killed in action, 10th April, 1918	—	France, 1918
RENTON, J. Mill	Captain	Major	Royal Army Medical Corps	—	Mentioned in Despatches	Egypt and Palestine, 1917–1918
RIDDEL, Charles David	Private	Lieutenant	Cameron Highlanders Royal Engineers	—	—	—
RIDDEL, Hinshaw-, Douglas C.	Despatch Rider	Corporal	Royal Engineers	—	—	France and Belgium, 1915–1916 Italy, 1917–1918 France, 1918
RIDDEL, John Alfred	Private	Lieutenant	Argyll & Sutherland Highlanders Tank Corps	—	—	—
RIDDELL, Brownlow	Captain	Lieut.-Colonel	Royal Army Medical Corps	—	Officer of the Order of the British Empire	Home Service

NAME.	RANK. At beginning of War or on joining.	RANK. At end of War.	UNIT.	CASUALTIES.	HONOURS OR DECORATIONS.	FIELD OF SERVICE.
RIDDELL, Malcolm Hendry	Cadet	2nd Lieutenant	Officer Cadet Battn. Royal Engineers Royal Air Force	—	—	—
RIDDELL, William John Brownlow	Midshipman	Midshipman	Royal Naval Volunteer Reserve	—	—	North Sea and English Channel, 1917–1918
✠ RIGG, Frederick	Gunner	Gunner	Royal Field Artillery	Killed in action, 30th September, 1917	—	France
RISK, James Douglas	Cadet	Cadet	Glasgow University Officers Training Corps	—	—	Home Service
✠ RITCHIE, J. J. Austin	2nd Lieutenant	2nd Lieutenant	9th (G.H.) Battn. Highland Light Infantry	Killed in action, 29th September, 1918	—	France, 1918
RITCHIE, J. Morrison	Surgeon Sub-Lieutenant	Surgeon Sub-Lieutenant	Royal Navy	—	—	At Sea, 1916–1917
✠ ROBB, Ralph George Campbell	Private	2nd Lieutenant	10th Battn. The Cameronians (Scottish Rifles)	Missing, presumed killed, 25/27th September, 1915, at Loos	—	France, 1915
ROBERTSON, Alick Page Anderson	Lieutenant	Lieutenant	6th Battn. The Black Watch (Royal Highlanders)	—	—	France, 1918
ROBERTSON, Archibald Hope	Lieutenant	Lieutenant	Royal Naval Volunteer Reserve	—	—	France and Belgium, 1914–1915

NAME.	RANK. At beginning of War or on joining.	At end of War.	UNIT.	CASUALTIES.	HONOURS OR DECORATIONS.	FIELD OF SERVICE.
ROBERTSON, Graham Monteith	Private	2nd Lieutenant	Highland Light Infantry Royal Air Force	Prisoner of War	—	—
ROBERTSON, Hugh	Private	Staff Sergeant	Argyll & Sutherland Highlanders Seaforth Highlanders School of Musketry	Wounded	—	—
ROBERTSON, Ian Forbes	Cadet	Cadet	Glasgow University Officers Training Corps	—	—	Home Service
ROBERTSON, John	Lieutenant	Lieutenant	8th Battn. Argyll & Sutherland Highlanders	Wounded twice	—	France, 1916 and 1918
ROBERTSON, John Alexander	Private	Captain	Highland Light Infantry	Invalided	—	—
ROBERTSON, John Howard	Cadet	Lieutenant	Inns of Court Officers Training Corps Royal Army Ordnance Corps	—	—	Home Service
ROBERTSON, B. Hamilton, M.B.	Lieutenant	Captain	Royal Army Medical Corps	—	—	—
✠ ROBERTSON, Robert Horsburgh	Private	Corporal	14th London Regiment (London Scottish)	Killed in action, 6th May, 1915	—	France, 1914-1915

Name.	Rank. At beginning of War or on joining.	Rank. At end of War.	Unit.	Casualties.	Honours or Decorations.	Field of Service.
✠ ROBERTSON, Thomas Bollen Seath McGregor	Lieutenant	Lieutenant	Royal Navy	Lost in North Sea, January 1917	—	Channel Patrol
ROBERTSON, Walter	Private	2nd Lieutenant	Highland Light Infantry	—	—	—
✠ ROBERTSON, William Bruce	2nd Lieutenant	2nd Lieutenant	8th Battn. The Cameronians (Scottish Rifles)	Killed in action, 28th June, 1915	—	Gallipoli, 1915
ROBIN, Robert Douglas	Captain	Captain	9th (G.H.) Battn. Highland Light Infantry	—	—	France, 1918
✠ ROBINSON, Harold Robert	2nd Lieutenant	2nd Lieutenant	Royal Garrison Artillery	Killed, 13th October, 1918, at Le Cateau	—	France, 1918
ROBINSON, John Dixon	Lieutenant	Lieutenant	Service de Santé and Royal Army Medical Corps	—	—	France, 1916–1918
RODGER, John K.	Cadet	2nd Lieutenant	Glasgow University Officers Training Corps The Cameronians (Scottish Rifles)	—	—	Home Service
RODGER, Lawton Keir	Private	Lieutenant	Royal Engineers	Invalided, August 1916	—	Egypt, 1916
RODGER, William Keir	2nd Lieutenant	Lieutenant	4th Battn. The Cameronians (Scottish Rifles)	Wounded, August 1916 Wounded, November 1917	—	Gallipoli, 1915 Egypt, Sinai, Palestine, 1916–1918
ROEMMELE, Alfred	Captain	Captain	Royal Army Medical Corps	—	—	Salonika, 1917–1918

NAME.	RANK. At beginning of War or on joining.	RANK. At end of War.	UNIT.	CASUALTIES.	HONOURS OR DECORATIONS.	FIELD OF SERVICE.
ROEMMELE, Harold A.	2nd Lieutenant	2nd Lieutenant	General List	Invalided, 1914	—	Home Service
ROEMMELE, Herman M.	Lieutenant	Captain	Royal Army Veterinary Corps	—	—	Home Service
ROEMMELE, Max Alexander	2nd Lieutenant	Captain	4th Battn. Queen's Own Cameron Highlanders	—	Mentioned in Despatches	France and Belgium, 1915–1916
✠ ROLLAND, Charles Douglas	Private	Lance-Corporal	17th Battn. Highland Light Infantry	Killed in action, 1st July, 1916, on the Somme	—	France, 1916
✠ ROLLAND, Frederick James Gordon	2nd Lieutenant	Lieutenant	6th Battn. King's Own Scottish Borderers	Killed in action, 25th September, 1915, at Loos	—	France, 1915
ROLLAND, Ralph A.	2nd Lieutenant	2nd Lieutenant	Royal Garrison Artillery	—	—	France, 1918
ROSE, Alexander Allistair	Lieutenant	Lieutenant	The Cameronians (Scottish Rifles) Royal Engineers	—	—	—
✠ ROSE, Andrew Mackenzie	Private	Private	Australian Imperial Forces	Wounded and prisoner, 15th April, 1918, at Hangard Wood Died from wounds on 25th April, 1918	—	Gallipoli, 1915 France, 1918
ROSE, Arthur Osborne	Private	Lance-Corporal	17th Battn. Highland Light Infantry	Wounded, September 1916	—	France, 1916–1918

NAME.	RANK. At beginning of War or on joining.	RANK. At end of War.	UNIT.	CASUALTIES.	HONOURS OR DECORATIONS.	FIELD OF SERVICE.
ROSE, James Morton	Colour-Sergeant	Colour-Sergeant	Rangoon Rifles	—	—	—
ROSE, John Alexander	Cadet	Cadet	17th Battn. Highland Light Infantry	Wounded, July 1916	—	France, 1916
ROSE, Lewis	Cadet	Lieutenant	Inns of Court Officers Training Corps; 3rd Battn. Seaforth Highlanders	Invalided, January 1918	—	France, 1916-1918
✠ ROSE, Richmond	Bombardier	Bombardier	Royal Field Artillery	Died of Dysentery, 12th October, 1915, at Malta	—	Gallipoli, 1915
ROSS, Bertram	Private	Lieutenant	9th (G.H.) Battn. Highland Light Infantry	Wounded, May 1915	—	France, 1914-1918
ROSS, David	Private	Private	Honorable Artillery Company	—	—	Home Service
ROSS, Donald M.	Private	Private	Highland Light Infantry	Invalided	—	—
ROSS, John A.	Cadet	Cadet	Glasgow University Officers Training Corps	—	—	Home Service
✠ ROSS, William	Private	2nd Lieutenant	6th Battn. Highland Light Infantry; 9th (G.H.) Battn. Highland Light Infantry	Killed in action, April 1918	—	France
ROWAN, Harry B.	Lieutenant	Captain	Queen's Own Cameron Highlanders	Wounded, March 1916; Wounded, October 1916; Wounded, July 1917	Mentioned in Despatches; Military Cross	France, 1915-1918

Name.	Rank. At beginning of War or on joining.	Rank. At end of War.	Unit.	Casualties.	Honours or Decorations.	Field of Service.
ROXBURGH, George A.	Lieutenant	Lieutenant	Central India Horse, (Indian Army)	—	—	—
✠ ROXBURGH, John Wood	2nd Lieutenant	Lieutenant	Royal Scots Fusiliers	Killed in action, 19th April, 1917	—	France
ROXBURGH, Robert	2nd Lieutenant	Lieutenant	6th Battn. Highland Light Infantry	—	Military Cross	France, 1916–1917
RUDD, Arthur Howard	2nd Lieutenant	Flying Officer	Royal Flying Corps Royal Air Force	—	—	France, 1917–1918
RUDD, David Heylin	Private	Flying Officer	17th Battn. Highland Light Infantry Royal Field Artillery Royal Flying Corps	Wounded, March 1916	—	France, Belgium, 1915–1916 Egypt, 1916 Belgium, 1917
RUFF, F. Metcalfe	Lieutenant	Captain	22nd Punjabis	Invalided	—	North West Frontier
RUFF, Louis A.	Private	Sergeant	9th (G.H.) Battn. Highland Light Infantry	Wounded, May 1915	Belgian War Cross	France, 1914–1918
RUFF, Victor Shaw	Private	Lieutenant	5th Battn. The Cameronians (Scottish Rifles)	Invalided, September 1916	—	France, 1916 British East Africa, 1918
RUSSELL, Albert	Lieutenant	Lieutenant	Royal Engineers	—	—	Home Service
✠ RUSSELL, Arthur	Private	Lieutenant	9th (G.H.) Battn. Highland Light Infantry	Died of wounds, 16th July, 1916	—	France, 1915–1916

NAME.	RANK. At beginning of War or on joining.	RANK. At end of War.	UNIT.	CASUALTIES.	HONOURS OR DECORATIONS.	FIELD OF SERVICE.
RUSSELL, Bertie Angus	2nd Lieutenant	Captain	The Gloucestershire Regiment	Wounded, July 1917 Wounded, October, 1917 Wounded, August 1918	Mentioned in Despatches twice Distinguished Service Order	France, 1916–1918
RUSSELL, Edward A. S.	Private	Corporal	Royal Army Service Corps	—	—	France, 1918
RUSSELL, Frederick A.	Lieutenant	Lieutenant	17th Battn. Highland Light Infantry	—	Mentioned in Despatches	France, 1916–1918
✠ RUSSELL, Hamish Galbraith	2nd Lieutenant	2nd Lieutenant	7th Battn. Highland Light Infantry	Died of wounds, 16th July, 1915	—	Gallipoli, 1915
RUSSELL, Herbert Mannington	2nd Lieutenant	Captain	6th Battn. Highland Light Infantry	—	—	Gallipoli, 1915 Egypt, 1916–1918
RUSSELL, J. Vaughan	Sergeant	Staff Sergeant	Scottish Horse	—	—	Gallipoli, 1915 Palestine, 1916
✠ RUSSELL, James	Captain	Captain	17th Battn. Highland Light Infantry	Wounded, 1st July, 1916 Died, 10th July, 1917	Military Cross	France, 1915–1916
✠ RUSSELL, Peter Currie Stuart	2nd Lieutenant	Lieutenant	5th Battn. The Cameronians (Scottish Rifles) Royal Flying Corps	Killed in action, 19th December, 1915	—	France
✠ RUSSELL, Thomas	Lieutenant	Captain	5th Battn. The Cameronians (Scottish Rifles)	Killed in action, 19th April, 1916	—	France
✠ RUTHERFORD, Edward Paterson	2nd Lieutenant	Captain	5th Battn. Highland Light Infantry	Died on Service, 17th January, 1916	—	—

Name.	Rank. At beginning of War or on joining.	Rank. At end of War.	Unit.	Casualties.	Honours or Decorations.	Field of Service.
RUTHERFORD, Samuel	Captain	Captain	Royal Army Medical Corps	—	Military Cross	France and Belgium, 1917–1918
SANDEMAN, Archibald	Lieutenant	Captain	9th Battn. Argyll & Sutherland Highlanders	Invalided, September 1917	—	Home Service
SANDEMAN, David C.	Ambulance Driver	Air Mechanic	British Red Cross Society Royal Air Force	—	—	France, 1915–1916 and 1918
SANDEMAN, Frank Watt	Private	Captain	9th (G.H.) Battn. Highland Light Infantry	Invalided, June 1918	—	France, 1914–1915 Mesopotamia, 1917–1918
SANDEMAN, Harry Boswell	Private	Captain	9th Battn. Argyll & Sutherland Highlanders	Wounded and prisoner, March 1918	—	France, 1917–1918
SANDEMAN, John Milne	Private	Lieutenant	Argyll & Sutherland Highlanders Highland Light Infantry	Invalided, December 1916 Invalided, August 1918	—	France, 1916 Palestine and France, 1918
SANDFORD, Archibald L.	Private	Corporal	Cameron Highlanders Argyll & Sutherland Highlanders	—	—	—
SANDFORD, Arthur	Private	Private	Canadian Forces	—	—	—
SANDFORD, James Maclay	Private	Private	6th Battn. Gordon Highlanders	Invalided, August 1918	—	France, 1918
SANDFORD, John B.	Sergeant	Sergeant	5th Battn. The Cameronians (Scottish Rifles)	Wounded, October 1917	—	France, 1917–1918

NAME.	RANK. At beginning of War or on joining.	RANK. At end of War.	UNIT.	CASUALTIES.	HONOURS OR DECORATIONS.	FIELD OF SERVICE.
SAWERS, Thomas J.	Cadet	Cadet	Glasgow University Officers Training Corps	—	—	Home Service
SCLANDERS, Kenneth Gerald	Private	Captain	Royal Air Force,	Wounded	Mentioned in Despatches twice; Military Cross	France, 1914-1915; Palestine, 1915-1918
SCOTLAND, Patrick J.	Cadet	2nd Lieutenant	Glasgow University Officers Training Corps; The Black Watch (Royal Highlanders)	Wounded	—	—
SCOTT, Alexander Paterson	2nd Lieutenant	2nd Lieutenant	King's Own Scottish Borderers	—	—	—
SCOTT, Archibald Campbell	Cadet	Cadet	Glasgow University Officers Training Corps	—	—	Home Service
✠ SCOTT, Ralph Rookby	Private	Private	King's Own Scottish Borderers	Killed in action, 28th June, 1918	—	France
SCOTT, Wilfrid H.	Cadet	2nd Lieutenant	Officers Training Corps; Royal Flying Corps; Royal Air Force	—	—	—
✠ SCOUGAL, Alexander Graham	Private	Lieut.-Colonel	4th Battn. The Royal Scots (Royal Regiment)	Killed in action, 18th September, 1918	Military Cross	France, 1916-1918
✠ SCOUGAL, Frank William	Private	Major	The Cameronians (Scottish Rifles)	Killed in action, 19th September, 1918	Military Cross	France, 1915; Salonica, 1916-1918

I

NAME.	RANK. At beginning of War or on joining.	RANK. At end of War.	UNIT.	CASUALTIES.	HONOURS OR DECORATIONS.	FIELD OF SERVICE.
SCOULER, Alexander Buchanan	Sapper	Sapper	Royal Engineers	—	—	France and Belgium, 1916–1918
SEMPLE, James	Trooper	Lieutenant	Queen's Own Royal Glasgow Yeomanry. Royal Tank Corps	—	Military Cross	France, 1917–1918
✠ SERVICE, Alexander Cumming	Lieutenant	Captain	6th Battn. Argyll & Sutherland Highlanders Machine Gun Corps	Killed in action, 31st May, 1918, in Palestine	—	Mesopotamia, 1916; Egypt, 1918
SETTEN, Norman Silvester	Midshipman	Midshipman	Royal Naval Volunteer Reserve	—	—	Home Service
SHANKS, Alexander	Despatch Rider	Captain	6th Battn. Argyll & Sutherland Highlanders	Wounded, June, 1916	Military Cross	France and Belgium, 1915–1918
SHANKS, Gilbert McCallum	Private	Lieutenant	5th Battn. The Cameronians (Scottish Rifles)	Wounded, August, 1916	—	France, 1916
✠ SHANKS, John Arthur Gordon	Lieutenant	Captain	6th Battn. Argyll & Sutherland Highlanders	Killed in action 4th October, 1917	Mentioned in Despatches. Military Cross	France, 1915–1917
SHANKS, Ronald J.	Lieutenant	Captain	6th Battn. Argyll & Sutherland Highlanders	Wounded, March, 1916. Invalided, June, 1918	—	France, 1915–1916; German East Africa, 1917–1918
SHANKS, Seymour Cochrane	Lieutenant	Captain	Royal Army Medical Corps	—	—	Egypt, 1916; France, 1916
SHANKS, William	Private	Captain	6th Battn. Argyll & Sutherland Highlanders	Wounded, May, 1917	—	France, 1915–1917

NAME.	RANK. At beginning of War or on joining.	RANK. At end of War.	UNIT.	CASUALTIES.	HONOURS OR DECORATIONS.	FIELD OF SERVICE.
SHARP, Russell	Cadet	Cadet	Glasgow University Officers Training Corps	—	—	Home Service, 1918
SHAW, Archibald Douglas McInnes	2nd Lieutenant	Lieutenant-Colonel	7th Battn. Royal Scots Fusiliers 1st Battn. Royal Scots Fusiliers	Invalided, July, 1917 Invalided, January, 1918	Mentioned in Despatches twice Distinguished Service Order	France and Belgium, 1915–1918
SHEARER, Charles Nelson	2nd Lieutenant	2nd Lieutenant	8th Battn. Highland Light Infantry	Invalided, July, 1916	—	Home Service
SHERIFF, George	Private	Captain	14th Battn. The Royal Scots (Royal Regiment)	—	Mentioned in Despatches	India, 1916–1917 Mesopotamia, 1917–1918
SIMMONS, Edwin John Young	Sergeant	Captain	3rd (City of London) LondonRegiment (Royal Fusiliers)	Wounded, March, 1918 Wounded, June, 1918	—	France, 1917–1918
SIMPSON, Alexander F.	Sergeant	Lieutenant	5th Battn. Queen's Own Cameron Highlanders Machine Gun Corps	—	—	France, 1915 and 1918
SIMPSON, Herbert James Attwood	Private	2nd Lieutenant	Royal Army Medical Corps	—	—	—
SIMPSON, James Sieber Muir	Private	Lieutenant	28th (County of London) Battn. The London Regiment (Artists Rifles)	Invalided, June, 1917	—	France, 1917
SIMPSON, Maurice Muir	Private	Captain	Highland Light Infantry	Wounded, July, 1917	Military Cross	France and Belgium, 1916–1917

NAME.	RANK. At beginning of War or on joining.	RANK. At end of War.	UNIT.	CASUALTIES.	HONOURS OR DECORATIONS.	FIELD OF SERVICE.
SIMPSON, Raymond M. Muir	2nd Lieutenant	2nd Lieutenant	Royal Field Artillery, 3rd (Rangoon) Brigade	—	—	Rangoon, 1915-1917
SINCLAIR, David Horne	Lieutenant	Major	Canadian Corps of Signals	Wounded, April, 1915	—	France and Belgium, 1914-1918
✚ SINCLAIR, Eric Alexander	Private	2nd Lieutenant	9th (G.H.) Highland Light Infantry Royal Scots Fusiliers	Missing and presumed killed, 23rd April, 1917	—	France, 1917
✚ SINCLAIR, Herbert Spencer	2nd Lieutenant	2nd Lieutenant	Royal Flying Corps	Killed on Service, 24th December, 1917	—	—
SINCLAIR, James Patrick	Corporal	2nd Lieutenant	Royal Engineers	—	—	—
SINCLAIR, James Ronald Sheriff	Cadet	Midshipman	Edinburgh University Officers Training Corps Royal Naval Reserve	—	—	—
SINCLAIR, Robert John	2nd Lieutenant	Lieutenant	5th Battn. King's Own Scottish Borderers	Wounded, July, 1915	Mentioned in Despatches Member of the Order of the British Empire	Gallipoli, 1915
SLOAN, Alexander Bankier	Major	Major	Royal Army Medical Corps	Invalided, September, 1915	Mentioned in Despatches three times	Gallipoli, 1915 Egypt and Palestine, 1916-1918
SLOAN, George Findlay	2nd Lieutenant	Lieutenant	8th Battn. Argyll & Sutherland Highlanders	—	—	France, 1918

NAME.	RANK. At beginning of War or on joining.	RANK. At end of War.	UNIT.	CASUALTIES.	HONOURS OR DECORATIONS.	FIELD OF SERVICE.
SLOAN, Oswald Tennant	Private	Captain	8th Battn. The Cameronians (Scottish Rifles)	Wounded, June, 1915	—	Gallipoli, 1915
✠ SLOAN, Wilfrid Scott	2nd Lieutenant	Lieutenant	8th Battn. The Cameronians (Scottish Rifles)	Died of wounds, 28th April, 1917, at Camiers	—	France, 1917
SLOAN, William Newlands	2nd Lieutenant	Captain	8th Battn. The Cameronians (Scottish Rifles)	Wounded, 1915	—	Gallipoli, 1915
SMALL, Edward A.	Cadet	Cadet	Glasgow University Officers Training Corps	—	—	Home Service
SMELLIE, John	Private	Lieutenant	6th Battn. Argyll & Sutherland Highlanders	—	—	France, 1918
SMITH, A. B.	Private	Private	Highland Light Infantry	—	—	—
SMITH, Alexander Findlay Cairns	Lieutenant	Lieutenant	Royal Field Artillery	—	—	France, 1917–1918
SMITH, Alick Drummond Buchanan	Private	Lieutenant	Gordon Highlanders	—	—	France and Belgium, 1918
SMITH, Charles Adamson	Private	Lance-Corporal	Royal Army Ordnance Corps	—	—	France, 1917–1918
SMITH, Charles Mitchell	Lieutenant	Captain	Royal Engineers,	Invalided, 1917	—	France, 1917

Name.	Rank. At beginning of War or on joining.	Rank. At end of War.	Unit.	Casualties.	Honours or Decorations.	Field of Service.
SMITH, Douglas Pearson	Probationary Flight Officer	2nd Lieutenant	Royal Naval Air Service Royal Air Force	—	—	Home Service
SMITH, Ernest	Lieutenant	Captain	The Cameronians (Scottish Rifles)	—	—	—
SMITH, Ernest Forsyth	Corporal	Lieutenant	Royal Engineers	Invalided, 1915	—	France, 1915–1918
SMITH, G. Stanley	2nd Lieutenant	Captain	5th Battn. The Cameronians (Scottish Rifles)	Invalided, May, 1916	Military Cross	France, 1914–1916 and 1918 Palestine, 1917–1918
✠ SMITH, George Buchanan	2nd Lieutenant	2nd Lieutenant	Gordon Highlanders	Wounded, 14th December, 1914 Killed in action, 25th September, 1915, at Loos	Mentioned in Despatches	France, 1914–1915
✠ SMITH, Gordon Macleod	Private	Private	9th (G.H.) Battn. Highland Light Infantry	Accidentally killed, January, 1917, in France	—	France, 1916–1917
✠ SMITH, Herbert Fyfe	2nd Lieutenant	2nd Lieutenant	Royal Scots Fusiliers	Killed in action, 23rd April, 1917	—	France
SMITH, James Blair	2nd Lieutenant	2nd Lieutenant	Royal Flying Corps	—	—	—
✠ SMITH, James Douglas	Private	Captain	9th (G.H.) Battn. Highland Light Infantry 7th Battn. The Cameronians (Scottish Rifles)	Wounded, 1916 Killed in action, 27th September, 1918, at Moeuvres	—	Egypt, 1916–1917 France, 1918

Name.	Rank. At beginning of War on joining.	Rank. At end of War.	Unit.	Casualties.	Honours or Decorations.	Field of Service.
Smith, James Geddes	Private	Private	The Royal Fusiliers	—	—	—
✠ Smith, James Osbourne	Private	Lieutenant	Ayrshire Yeomanry 7th Battn. The Cameronians (Scottish Rifles)	Killed in action, 1st November, 1917	—	Gallipoli, 1915 Egypt, 1916–1917
Smith, John Arthur	Private	Captain	Australian Imperial Forces	Wounded, April, 1915 Invalided, 1917	—	Gallipoli, 1915 France, 1916–1917
Smith, John Sydney	Lieutenant	Captain	6th Battn. Highland Light Infantry	Wounded, March, 1917	—	Gallipoli, 1915 Egypt, 1916–1917
Smith, Reginald	Private	Private	Queen's Royal West Surrey Regiment	—	—	—
✠ Smith, Robert Dunlop	Lieutenant	Captain	33rd Punjabis, Indian Army	Killed in action, 12th June, 1917	—	East Africa, 1917
Smith, Robert Stanley	2nd Lieutenant	Lieutenant	7th Battn. Argyll & Sutherland Highlanders	Wounded Invalided	—	France, 1915–1918
Snodgrass, William Robertson	2nd Lieutenant	Captain	Royal Army Medical Corps	Invalided, 1917	—	France, 1915–1917 and 1918
Somerville, Colin F.	Lieutenant	Lieutenant	Royal Army Medical Corps	—	—	—
Somerville, Richard Kirkpatrick	Cadet	Cadet	Glasgow University Officers Training Corps	—	—	Home Service

Name.	Rank. At beginning of War or on joining.	Rank. At end of War.	Unit.	Casualties.	Honours or Decorations.	Field of Service.
SOMMERVILLE, William Francis	Lieut.-Colonel	Lieut.-Colonel	Royal Army Medical Corps	—	Mentioned in Despatches twice	Home Service
SOMMERVILLE, Alexander J.	Gunner	Gunner	Royal Garrison Artillery	Invalided	—	—
SOMMERVILLE, Malcolm	Lieutenant	Captain	Royal Army Medical Corps	Invalided, March, 1918	Mentioned in Despatches Military Cross	Gallipoli, 1915 Egypt and Palestine, 1916–1918 France, 1918
✠ SPEIRS, George Patrick	Lieutenant	Major	6th Battn. Highland Light Infantry	Wounded, 1916 Killed in action, 1st October, 1918	French War Cross	Gallipoli, 1915 Egypt, 1916-1917 France, 1918
SPEIRS, Hector McArthur	Flight Cadet	Flight Cadet	Royal Air Force	—	—	Home Service
SPEIRS, James	2nd Lieutenant	Captain	6th Battn. Highland Light Infantry	—	—	France, 1916 and 1918
SPEIRS, Ronald	2nd Lieutenant	Lieutenant	6th Battn. The Cameronians (Scottish Rifles)	Wounded, September, 1916	—	France and Belgium, 1915-1916 and 1918
SPENCE, John	2nd Lieutenant	Lieutenant	Argyll & Sutherland Highlanders	—	—	—
✠ SPENCE, Telford Francis	Private	Private	17th Battn. Highland Light Infantry	Killed in action, 1st July, 1916, on the Somme	—	France, 1916

Name.	Rank. At beginning of War or on joining.	Rank. At end of War.	Unit.	Casualties.	Honours or Decorations.	Field of Service.
✠ SPENS, William	Lieutenant	Lieutenant	9th (G.H.) Battn. Highland Light Infantry	Killed in action, 17th May, 1915, at Richebourg St. Vaast	—	France, 1914–1915
✠ SPENS, William Thomas Patrick	2nd Lieutenant	Lieutenant	The Royal Scots (Royal Regiment)	Died on Service, 18th February, 1917	—	France
SPIERS, George Claude	Cadet	2nd Lieutenant	Officer Cadet Battn. Argyll & Sutherland Highlanders	—	—	—
SPREULL, James Manly	Cadet	Lieutenant	Inns of Court Officers Training Corps 7th Battn. Highland Light Infantry	—	—	Egypt, 1916–1917 France, 1918
✠ STALKER, Francis Brown Douglas	2nd Lieutenant	2nd Lieutenant	—	Killed in action, 22nd August, 1915	—	Gallipoli, 1915
✠ STEELE, Francis Gardner	Private	2nd Lieutenant	7th Battn. Queen's Own Cameron Highlanders 18th Battn. Highland Light Infantry	Killed in action, 18th November, 1916, at Beaumont Hamel	—	France, 1915–1916
✠ STERLING, John Lockhart	Private	2nd Lieutenant	Highland Light Infantry Royal Scots Fusiliers	Killed in action, 28th September, 1915	—	France, 1915
✠ STERLING, Robert William	2nd Lieutenant	Lieutenant	Royal Scots Fusiliers	Killed in action, 23rd April, 1915	—	France, 1915

Name.	Rank. At beginning of War or on joining.	Rank. At end of War.	Unit.	Casualties.	Honours or Decorations.	Field of Service.
✠ STEVEN, George Gordon	Private	Lieutenant	6th Battn. The Queen's Own Cameron Highlanders Tank Corps	Killed in action, 24th October, 1916	—	France, 1916
STEVENS, Thomas S.	Cadet	Cadet	Glasgow University Officers Training Corps	—	—	Home Service
STEVENS, William A.	2nd Lieutenant	Lieutenant	Royal Inniskilling Fusiliers	—	—	—
✠ STEVENSON, Alan McDonald	2nd Lieutenant	Lieutenant	Royal Air Force	Killed in action, 5th April, 1918	—	Egypt, 1917-1918
STEVENSON, Alexander MacEwen	Chaplain 4th Class	Chaplain 3rd Class	Australian Expeditionary Force	—	Military Cross	Egypt, 1916-1917. France, 1918
STEVENSON, Andrew Kirkwood	2nd Lieutenant	Lieutenant	The Cameronians (Scottish Rifles)	Wounded, May, 1918	—	France, 1918
STEVENSON, Douglas Stuart	Lieutenant	Major	Royal Naval Volunteer Reserve Royal Air Force	—	Member of the Order of the British Empire Belgian War Cross	At Sea, 1914-1916. France and Belgium, 1917-1918
STEVENSON, George Hope	2nd Lieutenant	Lieutenant	4th Battn. The Oxfordshire & Buckinghamshire Light Infantry	—	—	France, 1918

NAME.	RANK. At beginning of War or on joining.	RANK. At end of War.	UNIT.	CASUALTIES.	HONOURS OR DECORATIONS.	FIELD OF SERVICE.
STEVENSON, George L.	Lieutenant	Captain	Royal Army Service Corps	—	—	—
STEVENSON, Ian T.	Sub-Lieutenant	Lieutenant	Royal Naval Volunteer Reserve	—	Officer of the Order of the British Empire	At Sea, 1914–1918
STEVENSON, T. Bruce	Cadet	Cadet	Glasgow University Officers Training Corps	—	—	Home Service
STEVENSON, William Hugh	2nd Lieutenant	Lieutenant	5th Battn. Highland Light Infantry 33rd Punjabis, Indian Army	—	—	India
✠ STEWART, Andrew Phillip	Private	Lieutenant	5th Battn. The Cameronians (Scottish Rifles) 9th Battn. King's Own Scottish Borderers	Wounded, 24th March, 1918	Military Cross	France, 1914–1918
STEWART, Duncan	Cadet	Lieutenant	Glasgow University Officers Training Corps Royal Field Artillery	Accidentally drowned, 2nd June, 1918 Wounded, 1918	—	France, 1918
✠ STEWART, George Watson	Private	Private	Gordon Highlanders	Killed in action, 21st November, 1917, at Cambrai	—	France
✠ STEWART, Harry Walter Bettsworth	Private	Lance-Corporal	5th Battn. Highland Light Infantry	Killed in action, 13th July, 1915	—	Gallipoli, 1915
✠ STEWART, Hugh	Private	Lieutenant	9th (G.H.) Battn. Highland Light Infantry 12th Battn. Highland Light Infantry	Killed in action, 25th March, 1918, at Maricourt	—	France, 1917–1918

Name.	Rank. At beginning of War or on joining.	Rank. At end of War.	Unit.	Casualties.	Honours or Decorations.	Field of Service.
STEWART, John	Cadet	2nd Lieutenant	Glasgow University Officers Training Corps Royal Engineers	—	—	—
STEWART, J. Ramsay	Lieutenant	Captain	7th Battn. Highland Light Infantry Royal Air Force	Wounded, July, 1918	—	Gallipoli, 1915 Egypt and Palestine, 1916–1917 France, 1918
STEWART, Robertson Buchanan	2nd Lieutenant	Lieutenant	Highland Light Infantry	—	—	—
✠ STEWART, Ronald James	2nd Lieutenant	2nd Lieutenant	1st Battn. Seaforth Highlanders	Died of wounds, 28th January, 1916	—	Mesopotamia
STEWART, Samuel	Sergeant Instructor	Sergeant Instructor	Army Gymnastic Staff	—	—	Home Service
STIELL, Edwyn J.	Private	Lieutenant	Royal Engineers	—	—	—
✠ STOUT, Thomas	2nd Lieutenant	Lieutenant	8th Battn. The Cameronians (Scottish Rifles)	Killed in action, 28th June, 1915	—	Gallipoli, 1915
STRACHAN, James Frederick	2nd Lieutenant	Lieutenant	7th Battn. Highland Light Infantry	Wounded, April, 1916 Wounded, August, 1918	Mentioned in Despatches	Gallipoli, 1915–1916 Egypt and Palestine, 1916–1918 France, 1918
STRACHAN, Robert Sutherland	Lieutenant	Lieutenant	Royal Army Medical Corps	—	—	India, 1917–1918

Name	Rank. At beginning of War or on joining.	Rank. At end of War.	Unit.	Casualties.	Honours or Decorations.	Field of Service.
STRAIN, Lawrence H.	Lieutenant	Commander	Royal Naval Volunteer Reserve	—	Mentioned in Despatches three times. Distinguished Service Cross. Officer of the Order of the British Empire. Commander of the Order of the Redeemer	France, 1914. North Sea, 1915. Gallipoli, 1915. Mediterranean, 1916-1918
STRANG, Samuel F.	Lieutenant	Lieutenant	Royal Naval Volunteer Reserve	Invalided, 1918	—	North Sea, 1914-1915. Aegean Turkish Coast, 1915-1918
STRATHIE, David Norman	Farrier Sergeant	Farrier Sergeant	Southern Provinces Mounted Rifles. Delhi Light Horse	—	—	India, 1914-1918
STRATHIE, William Johnston	2nd Lieutenant	Lieutenant	5th Battn. Argyll & Sutherland Highlanders	—	Mentioned in Despatches	France, 1917-1918
✠ STROUD, Eric Hubert Noel	Private	Lieutenant	17th Battn. Highland Light Infantry. Royal Air Force	Killed in action, 21st April, 1918	—	France and the East, 1916-1918
✠ STUART, John Charles	Private	2nd Lieutenant	8th Battn. Argyll & Sutherland Highlanders. 5th Battn. The Cameronians (Scottish Rifles)	Died of wounds, 23rd February, 1917	—	France, 1916-1917

Name.	Rank. At beginning of War or on joining.	Rank. At end of War.	Unit.	Casualties.	Honours or Decorations.	Field of Service.
STUART, MOODY-, Kenneth Andrew	Lieutenant	Major	Royal Garrison Artillery Royal Field Artillery	Invalided, December, 1914 Gassed, 1917	Mentioned in Despatches	France, 1917 Italy, 1917–1918
✝ STUART, Maurice Stevenson	Gentleman-Cadet	2nd Lieutenant	Royal Military College, Sandhurst The Black Watch (Royal Highlanders)	Killed in action, 15th June, 1918, at Meteren	—	France, 1918
STUART, Robert Norman	2nd Lieutenant	Captain	7th Battn. The Cameronians (Scottish Rifles)	Wounded, July, 1915 Wounded, December, 1917	—	Gallipoli, 1915–1916 Egypt and Palestine, 1916–1918
✝ SUTHERLAND, Andrew Niel	Chaplain 2nd Class	Chaplain 2nd Class	Royal Army Chaplains Department	Died on Service, 1918	—	Home Service
SUTHERLAND, George Stewart	Private	Lieutenant	Queen's Own Cameron Highlanders Army Cyclist Corps Middlesex Regiment	—	—	—
✝ SUTHERLAND, John McIntyre	2nd Lieutenant	2nd Lieutenant	9th Battn. The Royal Scots (Royal Regiment)	Killed in action, 23rd April, 1917	—	France
SWAN, William George	Private	Lieutenant	9th (G.H.) Battn. Highland Light Infantry 1st Battn. Royal Scots Fusiliers	Wounded, March, 1915 Wounded, September, 1915 Wounded, July, 1916 Wounded, December, 1916	—	France, 1914–1916

Name.	Rank. At beginning of War or on joining.	Rank. At end of War.	Unit.	Casualties.	Honours or Decorations.	Field of Service.
SYME, William Smith	Private	Captain	6th Battn. Queen's Own Cameron Highlanders. 11th Battn. The Cheshire Regiment. 2/19th Punjabis	Invalided, June, 1916. Wounded, 1918	Military Cross	France, 1915-1918
TAGGART, Henry Rawson	Private	Lieutenant	17th Battn. Highland Light Infantry	Wounded, 1917. Invalided, October, 1918	—	Gallipoli, Egypt, Palestine, France, 1915-1918
✠ TAGGART, Henry Rawson	2nd Lieutenant	2nd Lieutenant	3rd Battn. Argyll & Sutherland Highlanders	Killed in action, 24th July, 1918	—	France, 1918
TAGGART, Herbert George	Corporal	Corporal	1st Canadian Machine Gun Battn.	—	—	France, 1916-1918
TAIT, James Douglas	2nd Lieutenant	Lieutenant	9th Battn. The Cameronians (Scottish Rifles)	Wounded, August, 1918	Military Cross	France, 1917-1918
✠ TAYLOR, Alexander	Lieutenant	Captain	The Royal Scots (Royal Regiment)	Killed in action, 21st April, 1917	—	France
TAYLOR, Bruce Hector	Cadet	Cadet	Glasgow University Officers Training Corps	—	—	Home Service
✠ TAYLOR, Edward Graham	Private	Lieutenant	7th Battn. Queen's Own Cameron Highlanders	Killed in action, 25th September, 1915, at Loos	—	France, 1915
✠ TAYLOR, Edward Graham	Private	Lieutenant	Highland Light Infantry	Died of wounds, 23rd May, 1917, at Etaples	—	France, 1916-1917

NAME.	RANK. At beginning of War or on joining.	RANK. At end of War.	UNIT.	CASUALTIES.	HONOURS OR DECORATIONS.	FIELD OF SERVICE.
TAYLOR, Edwin Osborne	Private	Private	Lovat's Scouts.	—	—	—
TAYLOR, George	Lieutenant	Captain	Royal Army Medical Corps	—	—	Egypt, 1917–1918
TAYLOR, James Anderson Kells	2nd Lieutenant	Captain	8th Battn. The Border Regiment 6th Dragoon Guards	Invalided, December, 1916	—	France, 1916 and 1918
TAYLOR, James McEwan Thomson	Private	Lieutenant	6th Battn. Queen's Own Cameron Highlanders	Wounded, August, 1918	Military Cross Bar to Military Cross	France, 1917–1918
TAYLOR, John Orr	Lieutenant	Major	4th Battn. The Royal Scots (Royal Regiment)	Wounded, April, 1917 Wounded, November, 1917	—	Gallipoli, Egypt and Palestine, 1915–1918
TAYLOR, Murray Ross	Captain	Lieut.-Colonel	Royal Army Medical Corps	Wounded, October, 1918	Mentioned in Despatches twice Distinguished Service Order	France, 1914–1918
TAYLOR, Ormond J.	2nd Lieutenant	2nd Lieutenant	Royal Army Service Corps	—	—	—
TAYLOR, William Crookenden	2nd Lieutenant	2nd Lieutenant	Highland Light Infantry	—	—	—
TAYLOR, William G.	Private	Private	Queen's Own Cameron Highlanders	—	—	Home Service

VICTORIA CROSS

" FOR most conspicuous bravery and resolution in the face of intense machine gun fire. During the initial advance he was shot through the right leg, but though crippled he continued to lead his men and captured the trench. In the captured trench Lieutenant Mackintosh collected men of another Company who had lost their leader and drove back a counter attack. He was again wounded, and although unable to stand he continued nevertheless to control the situation. With only fifteen men left he ordered his party to be ready to advance to the final objective, and with great difficulty got out of the trench and encouraged his men to advance. He was again wounded and fell. The gallantry and devotion to duty of this officer were beyond all praise ".

LIEUTENANT DONALD MACKINTOSH V.C.
SEAFORTH HIGHLANDERS

KILLED IN ACTION 11TH APRIL 1917

NAME.	RANK. At beginning of War on joining.	RANK. At end of War.	UNIT.	CASUALTIES.	HONOURS OR DECORATIONS.	FIELD OF SERVICE.
TEMPLETON, Andrew Ritchie	Private	Lieutenant	9th (G.H.) Battn. Highland Light Infantry 8th Battn. King's Own Scottish Borderers	Wounded, August 1917	—	France, 1915–1917
✠ TEMPLETON, Archibald Douglas	Lieutenant	Lieutenant	8th Battn. The Cameronians (Scottish Rifles)	Wounded and missing, 28th June, 1915	—	Gallipoli, 1915
TEMPLETON, Clement Bennet	Private	Private	6th Battn. Queen's Own Cameron Highlanders	Invalided, July 1918	—	France and Belgium, 1915–1918
✠ TEMPLETON, Godfrey Allan	Private	Lieutenant	7th Battn. Argyll & Sutherland Highlanders	Died of wounds, 24th July, 1918	—	France, 1918
TEMPLETON, John, Junr.	Private	1st Class Air Mechanic	Northumberland Fusiliers Royal Flying Corps	—	—	France, 1916–1918
TEMPLETON, Kenneth	2nd Lieutenant	Lieutenant	5th Battn. Seaforth Highlanders	.	—	France, 1918
TESSIER, Albert Louis	Sub-Lieutenant	Lieutenant	Royal Naval Reserve	—	Mentioned in Despatches	At Sea, 1914–1918
✠ THOM, Laurence Wilson	2nd Lieutenant	Lieutenant	8th Battn. The Cameronians (Scottish Rifles)	Died of wounds, 21st April, 1917	—	Egypt
THOMAS, George Vinson	2nd Lieutenant	Lieutenant	The Royal Fusiliers The East Yorkshire Regiment	—	Mentioned in Despatches Military Cross	—

K

Name.	Rank. At beginning of War or on joining.	At end of War.	Unit.	Casualties.	Honours or Decorations.	Field of Service.
THOMLINSON, William G.	Private	Lieutenant	9th (G.H.) Battn. Highland Light Infantry	—	—	France, 1916–1918
THOMPSON, W. D. Cargill	Cadet	Lieutenant	Glasgow University Officers Training Corps; 1st Battn. The Border Regiment	Wounded, November 1917	—	France, 1917
THOMSON, Aidan Gordon Wemyss	Lieutenant	Captain	Royal Army Medical Corps	Invalided, 1915	—	Mediterranean Expeditionary Force, 1915; Malta, 1917–1918
THOMSON, Alexander	2nd Lieutenant	2nd Lieutenant	South Wales Borderers	—	—	—
THOMSON, Donald F. S.	Private	Private	6th Battn. Queen's Own Cameron Highlanders	Wounded, September 1915; Invalided, March 1916	—	France, 1915
✠ THOMSON, Duncan Turner	Private	Private	9th (G.H.) Battn. Highland Light Infantry	Died of wounds, 30th July, 1915	—	France, 1914–1915
THOMSON, Gilbert E.	Private	Private	10th Battn. The Royal Scots (Royal Regiment)	—	—	Northern Russia, 1918
THOMSON, Harald D.	Private	2nd Lieutenant	Highland Light Infantry; Royal Engineers	Wounded	—	—
THOMSON, Henry William Hamilton	Private	Lieutenant	Highland Light Infantry; The Royal Scots (Royal Regiment)	Wounded	—	—
✠ THOMSON, James	Captain	Major	Royal Garrison Artillery	Invalided, October 1917; Died, 26th November, 1917	Mentioned in Despatches	France, 1915; Macedonia, 1916–1917

NAME.	RANK. At beginning of War or on joining.	At end of War.	UNIT.	CASUALTIES.	HONOURS OR DECORATIONS.	FIELD OF SERVICE.
THOMSON, James Cornwallis	Private	Captain	17th Battn. Highland Light Infantry	Invalided, March 1918	—	France and Belgium, 1915–1918
THOMSON, John A. G.	Chaplain	Chaplain	Royal Army Chaplains Department	—	—	France, 1917–1918
THOMSON, John Meason	Cadet	2nd Lieutenant	Glasgow University Officers Training Corps Royal Garrison Artillery	—	—	—
✠ THOMSON, Peter MacLellan	Lieutenant	Captain	5th Battn. Highland Light Infantry	Killed in action, 24th December, 1915, at Cape Helles	—	Gallipoli, 1915
THOMSON, R. Noel	Lieutenant	Captain	Royal Army Medical Corps	—	—	Home Service
THOMSON, W. D. Wood	Private	Private	15th Battn. The Cameronians (Scottish Rifles)	—	—	Home Service
✠ THOMSON, William	2nd Lieutenant	2nd Lieutenant	The Cameronians (Scottish Rifles)	Died on Service, 19th January, 1917	—	—
THOMSON, William I.	Private	Private	Royal Army Service Corps	—	—	Mesopotamia, 1916–1918 Persia, 1918
THORBURN, Sydney B.	Lance-Corporal	Lance-Corporal	The Cameronians (Scottish Rifles)	Wounded, April 1917	—	France, 1917
✠ TINDAL, David	Private	Private	17th Battn. Highland Light Infantry	Died of wounds, 30th June, 1916	—	France, 1915–1916

NAME.	RANK. At beginning of War or on joining	RANK. At end of War.	UNIT.	CASUALTIES.	HONOURS OR DECORATIONS.	FIELD OF SERVICE.
TODD, Matthew Gilmour	Private	2nd Lieutenant	Highland Light Infantry Machine-Gun Corps	—	—	—
TODD, Robert Taylor	Lieutenant	Captain	Royal Army Medical Corps	—	—	France, 1915–1917 Palestine and Egypt, 1917–1918
TORRANCE, Percy Watt	Lieutenant	Captain	Highland Light Infantry	—	Mentioned in Despatches Military Cross Legion of Honour 5th Class	—
TORRANCE, W. R. Duff	2nd Lieutenant	Captain	12th Battn. Argyll & Sutherland Highlanders	—	—	France, 1915 Salonika, 1915–1917 India, 1917
TULLIS, J. Kennedy	Major	Lieut.-Colonel	7th Battn. Argyll & Sutherland Highlanders	Wounded, May 1915	—	France, 1914–1915
✠ TULLIS, Robert Ramsey	Captain	Captain	7th Battn. Argyll & Sutherland Highlanders	Killed in action, 25th May, 1915	—	France, 1914–1915
TURNBULL, Alexander	2nd Lieutenant	2nd Lieutenant	Queen's Own Cameron Highlanders Army Cyclists' Corps	—	—	—
TURNBULL, Arthur	Lieutenant	Captain	Royal Army Medical Corps	—	—	France and Belgium, 1915 and 1918
TURNBULL, John W. G.	Assistant Paymaster	Assistant Paymaster	Royal Naval Volunteer Reserve	—	—	—

NAME.	RANK. At beginning of War or on joining.	RANK. At end of War.	UNIT.	CASUALTIES.	HONOURS OR DECORATIONS.	FIELD OF SERVICE
TURNER, William King	Sapper	Lance-Corporal	Royal Engineers	—	—	—
VALLANCE, H. L.	Private	Private	Highland Light Infantry	—	—	—
VANNAN, R. J.	Private	Private	Gloucestershire Regiment	—	—	Home Service
VEREL, James T. R.	Private	Lieutenant	Royal Flying Corps; The Border Regiment	Wounded, April 1918	—	France
VEREL, John A.	Private	Flight Cadet	Argyll & Sutherland Highlanders; Royal Air Force	—	—	Home Service
VINCENT, Clarence J.	Private	2nd Lieutenant	Inns of Court Officers Training Corps; The East Yorkshire Regiment	—	—	—
VINCENT, Herbert G.	Private	Private	Argyll & Sutherland Highlanders	—	—	—
✠ WADDELL, David Bruce	Gentleman-Cadet	2nd Lieutenant	Royal Military College, Sandhurst; 2nd Dragoon Guards (Queen's Bays)	Killed in action, 21st March, 1918, at Vendelles	—	France, 1918
WADDELL, Robert	Cadet	2nd Lieutenant	Officer Cadet Battn.	—	—	Home Service
WADDELL, Robert B.	Lieutenant	Captain	9th (G.H.) Battn. Highland Light Infantry	—	—	East Africa, 1917-1918

Name.	Rank. At beginning of War or on joining.	Rank. At end of War.	Unit.	Casualties.	Honours or Decorations.	Field of Service.
WADDELL, Roy	Cadet	Cadet	23rd Officer Cadet Battn.	—	—	Home Service
WADDELL, William Alastair	2nd Lieutenant	Captain	9th (G.H.) Battn. Highland Light Infantry	—	—	East Africa, 1916–1918
WALKER, Bryden Maitland	Private	2nd Lieutenant	Highland Light Infantry The Cameronians (Scottish Rifles)	—	—	—
WALKER, David Paterson	Midshipman	Midshipman	Royal Naval Volunteer Reserve	—	—	—
WALKER, Fred W.	Private	Private	14th Battn. London Regiment (London Scottish)	—	—	—
WALKER, George Bruce	Private	2nd Lieutenant	Highland Light Infantry Royal Flying Corps	Invalided	—	—
WALKER, Hugh R.	2nd Lieutenant	Lieutenant	9th (G.H.) Battn. Highland Light Infantry	—	—	East Africa, 1917–1918
WALKER, James M.	Private	Private	9th (G.H.) Battn. Highland Light Infantry	Wounded, September 1917 and Prisoner of War	—	France and Belgium, 1916–1917
WALKER, James Stuart	2nd Lieutenant	Captain	Highland Light Infantry Army Cyclist Corps	Invalided, August 1918	—	France, 1914–1918
WALKER, Robert	Air Mechanic	Air Mechanic	Royal Air Force	—	—	Home Service

Name.	Rank. At beginning of War or on joining.	Rank. At end of War	Unit.	Casualties.	Honours or Decorations.	Field of Service.
WALKER, Robert	Major	Major	Royal Army Service Corps Army Remounts	—	—	Home Service
WALKER, Robert W.	Private	2nd Lieutenant	Argyll & Sutherland Highlanders Highland Light Infantry	Wounded	—	—
WALKER, Thomas M.	Captain	Major	Royal Field Artillery	Invalided, September 1916	Mentioned in Despatches three times Distinguished Service Order	Gallipoli, 1915 France and Italy, 1917–1918
WALKER, William Norman	2nd Lieutenant	Captain	Royal Field Artillery	Invalided, 1917 and 1918	Military Cross	France, 1915–1918
WALLACE, Thomas Harold	Cadet	Cadet	Inns of Court Officers Training Corps	—	—	Home Service
✠ WALLACE, William Douglas	Private	2nd Lieutenant	The Cameronians (Scottish Rifles) Highland Light Infantry	Killed in action, 22nd August, 1916	—	France
WARR, Alfred E.	Private	Major	16th Battn. The Royal Scots (Royal Regiment)	Prisoner of War, April 1918	—	France, 1916–1918
WARR, Charles L.	2nd Lieutenant	2nd Lieutenant	9th Battn. Argyll & Sutherland Highlanders	Wounded, May 1915 Invalided, April 1916	—	Flanders, 1915
✠ WARREN, Alastair Bruce	Private	Private	17th Battn. Highland Light Infantry	Missing, 1st July, 1916	—	France, 1916

Name	Rank — At beginning of War or on joining	Rank — At end of War	Unit	Casualties	Honours or Decorations	Field of Service
WARREN, George Howden	Private	Lieutenant	9th (G.H.) Battn. Highland Light Infantry	—	—	—
WARREN, John Russell	2nd Lieutenant	Major	Royal Engineers	Wounded, May 1915 Wounded, September 1915 Wounded, March 1918	Mentioned in Despatches Military Cross	France, 1915–1918
WARREN, Ronald Crawford	Cadet	Cadet	Glasgow University Officers Training Corps	—	—	Home Service
WARREN, T. Allan	Private	Private	9th (G.H.) Battn. Highland Light Infantry	Wounded Invalided	—	France
✠ WARREN, Timothy Wilfred	Air Mechanic	Air Mechanic	Royal Flying Corps	Died, 16th March, 1917, at Aldershot	—	Home Service
✠ WATERSTON, John Knox	Private	Private	Cameron Highlanders	Killed in action	—	France
WATSON, Cecil	Private	Gunner	The Royal Fusiliers Army Cyclists Corps Tank Corps	—	—	—
✠ WATSON, David Henry	Private	Lance-Corporal	New Zealand Expeditionary Forces	Invalided, 1915 Killed in action, 1st October, 1916, on the Somme	—	Gallipoli, 1915 France, 1916
✠ WATSON, Laurence Stewart	2nd Lieutenant	Lieutenant	8th Battn. The Cameronians (Scottish Rifles)	Killed in action, 31st July, 1918, at Beauleux	—	Egypt, 1916–1917 France, 1918

NAME.	RANK. At beginning of War or on joining.	RANK. At end of War.	UNIT.	CASUALTIES.	HONOURS OR DECORATIONS.	FIELD OF SERVICE.
✠ WATSON, Louden	Gunner	Gunner	Royal Tank Corps	Killed in action, 22nd August, 1918	—	France
WATT, Bertram	Sapper	Sapper	Royal Engineers	—	—	—
WATT, James	Private	Private	Canadian Expeditionary Forces	—	—	—
WATT, John Alexander	Cadet	2nd Lieutenant	Officer Cadet Battn. The Cameronians (Scottish Rifles	Wounded and Prisoner of War	—	—
WATT, John Cunningham	2nd Lieutenant	2nd Lieutenant	Royal Flying Corps	—	—	—
WATT, Thomas	Lieutenant	Captain	The Cameronians (Scottish Rifles)	Wounded	—	—
WATT, Thomas Charles Dalrymple	2nd Lieutenant	Captain	Royal Army Medical Corps	Wounded, March 1918	Military Cross	France, 1917-1918
WATT, Vincent J. B.	Cadet	Cadet	Glasgow University Officers Training Corps	—	—	Home Service
WATT, William J. C.	Surgeon Probationer	Surgeon	Royal Navy	—	—	At Sea, 1916-1918
WEBSTER, James D.	Private	Private	17th Battn. Highland Light Infantry Royal Engineers	—	—	—
✱ WEBSTER, R. W. Gordon	Private	Private	Gordon Highlanders	Killed in action, 23rd August, 1918	—	France, 1918

NAME.	RANK.		UNIT.	CASUALTIES.	HONOURS OR DECORATIONS.	FIELD OF SERVICE.
	At beginning of War or on joining.	At end of War.				
WEIR, Cecil McAlpine	2nd Lieutenant	Captain	7th Battn. The Cameronians (Scottish Rifles)	Wounded, July 1915	Mentioned in Despatches twice Military Cross	Gallipoli, 1915 France, 1916–1918
WEIR, Ian Everest Rose	2nd Lieutenant	Captain	126th Baluchistan Infantry (Indian Army)	Wounded, January 1917	—	Egypt, Arabia, Baluchistan, Mesopotamia, 1914–1918
WEIR, James Leslie Rose	Captain	Lieut.-Colonel	5th Cavalry, Indian Army	—	2nd Class of the Persian Order of the Lion and the Sun	India, 1917 Mesopotamia, 1917–1918 N. Persia, 1918
WEIR, Patrick W. R.	Lieutenant	Lieutenant	Royal Navy	—	—	At Sea, 1914–1918
WELLS, Robert Tait	Captain	Captain	Indian Medical Service	—	—	—
WHALL, Cecil L. B.	Sergeant	Captain	The Royal Fusiliers Durham Light Infantry	Invalided, 1916	—	France, 1915–1916
WHIMSTER, Henry N.	Lieutenant	Lieutenant	6th Battn. Argyll & Sutherland Highlanders	Wounded, July 1916	—	France, 1916–1918
WHITE, Alexander L.	Staff-Sergeant	Lieutenant	Canadian Army Service Corps Royal Garrison Artillery	—	—	France, 1915–1916 France, 1918
WHITE, Charles E. P.	Private	Private	Lancashire Fusiliers	—	—	—
WHITE, George	Private	Private	Highland Light Infantry	—	—	—

NAME.	RANK. At beginning of War or on joining.	RANK. At end of War.	UNIT.	CASUALTIES.	HONOURS OR DECORATIONS.	FIELD OF SERVICE.
✠ WHITE, John Gardner	2nd Lieutenant	Lieutenant	5th Battn. The Cameronians (Scottish Rifles) Royal Flying Corps	Killed in action, 26th August, 1917	—	France
WHITE, John Mair	Cadet	Lieutenant	Officer Cadet School Royal Field Artillery	Wounded, October 1918	—	France and Belgium, 1918
WHITE, Kennedy	Gunner	Gunner	Royal Field Artillery	—	—	Home Service
WHITE, Matthew	Lieutenant	Captain	Royal Army Medical Corps	—	—	Italy, 1918
WHITE, Robert M.	2nd Lieutenant	2nd Lieutenant	Argyll & Sutherland Highlanders	Invalided	—	—
WHITE, William	Corporal	Corporal	The Cameronians (Scottish Rifles)	—	—	—
WHITE, William D.	Private	2nd Lieutenant	The Cameronians (Scottish Rifles) Highland Light Infantry	Wounded Prisoner	—	—
WHITE, William J. M.	Lieutenant	Lieutenant	Royal Army Medical Corps	—	—	—
WHITELAW, Charles Edward	Captain	Captain	5th Battn. The Cameronians (Scottish Rifles)	—	—	Home Service
WHITELAW, H. Vincent	Captain	Captain	The Sherwood Foresters (Nottinghamshire and Derbyshire Regiment)	Invalided, 1918	—	Egypt, 1917–1918

Name.	Rank. At beginning of War or on joining.	Rank. At end of War.	Unit.	Casualties.	Honours or Decorations.	Field of Service.
WHITSON, Ernest J.	Captain	Captain	9th (G.H.) Battn. Highland Light Infantry	—	Mentioned in Despatches; Military Cross	France, 1915–1918
WHITSON, Gilbert Carrick	2nd Lieutenant	Captain	Royal Field Artillery,	—	Mentioned in Despatches	Egypt, 1916–1918
WHITSON, Ralph Alexander	2nd Lieutenant	Captain	Royal Field Artillery,	—	Mentioned in Despatches	Egypt, 1916–1917
✠ WHITSON, Wilfred Robert	Lieutenant	Major	9th (G.H.) Battn. Highland Light Infantry; The Suffolk Regiment	Killed in action, 30th November, 1917	—	France, 1914–1917
WHYTE, Hartley Waddington	2nd Lieutenant	Captain	The Royal Tank Corps	—	Mentioned in Despatches; Military Cross	France and Belgium, 1917–1918
WHYTE, James T. A.	Private	Private	9th Battn. The Black Watch (Royal Highlanders)	Wounded, April 1918	—	France, 1916–1918
WILKIE, Herbert E.	2nd Lieutenant	Captain	7th Battn. The Black Watch (Royal Highlanders)	Invalided, January 1918	—	France, 1915–1918
WILLIAMS, Llewellyn	Sergeant	Sergeant	Australian Cavalry	Wounded	—	—
WILLIAMSON, Alexander	2nd Lieutenant	Captain	4th Battn. The Cameronians (Scottish Rifles)	Wounded, July 1917	—	France, 1916–1917

NAME.	RANK. At beginning of War or on joining.	RANK. At end of War.	UNIT.	CASUALTIES.	HONOURS OR DECORATIONS.	FIELD OF SERVICE.
WILSON, Fred J. C.	Lieutenant	Lieutenant	The Cameronians (Scottish Rifles)	—	—	—
WILSON, Frederick Arnold	2nd Lieutenant	Captain	The Cameronians (Scottish Rifles)	—	Mentioned in Despatches	—
WILSON, George Nairn	2nd Lieutenant	2nd Lieutenant	6th Battn. Highland Light Infantry	Wounded, July 1915	—	Gallipoli, 1915
WILSON, Gordon	Private	Private	Royal Army Service Corps	Invalided, August 1917	—	Home Service
WILSON, Hamish	Private	Lieutenant	Queen's Own Cameron Highlanders Royal Flying Corps	Wounded Invalided	—	—
WILSON, Harry Archibald	Cadet	Cadet	Royal Flying Corps School	—	—	—
WILSON, Harry Ellis Charter	Cadet	2nd Lieutenant	Officer Cadet Battn. 9th Battn. Argyll & Sutherland Highlanders	—	—	Home Service
WILSON, Henry Noel	Private	2nd Lieutenant	Inns of Court Officers Training Corps Royal Engineers	—	—	—

Name.	Rank. At beginning of War or on joining.	Rank. At end of War.	Unit.	Casualties.	Honours or Decorations.	Field of Service.
✠ WILSON, Michael Connal	Private	2nd Lieutenant	9th (G.H.) Battn. Highland Light Infantry 8th Battn. The Cameronians (Scottish Rifles)	Killed in action, 20th July, 1916, at High Wood	—	France, 1914–1916
WILSON, Noël	Driver	Lieutenant	Royal Field Artillery	Invalided, March 1918	—	France and Belgium, 1917–1918
WILSON, Patrick Hogarth	Captain	Lieutenant-Colonel	Royal Field Artillery	—	Mentioned in Despatches Distinguished Service Order Brevet Lieut.-Colonel	France, 1915–1916
WILSON, Robert Macnair	Lieutenant	Lieutenant	Royal Army Medical Corps Royal Engineers	—	—	—
WILSON, Roy Young	Sapper	Lieutenant	Royal Engineers Royal Flying Corps	—	—	France, 1914–1915 Russia, September 1918
WILSON, W. S. B.	Lieutenant	Lieutenant	The Cameronians (Scottish Rifles)	—	—	—
WILSON, William Mitchell Turner	Lieutenant	Captain	Royal Army Medical Corps	—	—	France and Belgium, 1917–1918
WINNING, Herbert	1st Air Mechanic	1st Air Mechanic	Royal Flying Corps	—	—	—
WOOD, Hugh Evelyn	Private	2nd Lieutenant	10th Battn. Argyll & Sutherland Highlanders	Invalided, December 1916	—	Salonika, 1916–1917

NAME.	RANK. At beginning of War or on joining.	At end of War.	UNIT.	CASUALTIES.	HONOURS OR DECORATIONS.	FIELD OF SERVICE.
WOOD, James A.	2nd Lieutenant	Lieutenant	Royal Army Medical Corps. 1st Lowland Field Ambulance	Invalided, November 1916 Wounded, October 1918	—	Gallipoli, 1915 Belgium, Italy, France, 1917-1918
WOOD-SMITH, Norman	Lieutenant	Lieutenant-Commander	Royal Navy	—	—	France, 1914 Egypt, 1915-1916 India and Mesopotamia, 1917-1918
WORDIE, James Mann	2nd Lieutenant	Lieutenant	Royal Field Artillery	Wounded, April 1918	—	France, 1918
WORDIE, William	Captain	Major	Royal Army Service Corps	—	Mentioned in Despatches three times Officer of the Order of the British Empire Order of the Nile, 4th Class Order of the Nahda, 4th Class	Gallipoli and Salonika, 1915-1916 Egypt, 1917-1918
✠ WORKMAN, Charles Service	2nd Lieutenant	Lieutenant	5th Battn. The Cameronians (Scottish Rifles) Royal Flying Corps	Died of wounds, 20th July, 1917	Military Cross	France, 1914-1917
WOTHERSPOON, Gilbert	Private	2nd Lieutenant	The Cameronians (Scottish Rifles) Highland Light Infantry	—	—	—

NAME.	RANK. At beginning of War or on joining.	RANK. At end of War.	UNIT.	CASUALTIES.	HONOURS OR DECORATIONS.	FIELD OF SERVICE.
WOTHERSPOON, James Thomson	2nd Lieutenant	Lieutenant	Royal Scots Fusiliers	Wounded, September 1916 Wounded, October 1918	—	France, 1916 Salonika, 1917–1918
WRIGHT, Albert Edward	Private	Lieutenant	Royal Army Service Corps	Invalided, December 1917	—	France, 1917–1918 Serbia, 1918
WRIGHT, Gordon Mitchell	Private	Private	9th (G.H.) Battn. Highland Light Infantry	Wounded, May 1915	—	France and Belgium, 1914–1915
WRIGHT, John Bennett	Private	Lieutenant	Queen's Own Cameron Highlanders	Wounded, July 1916 Invalided, October 1918	—	France, 1915–1916 and 1918
WYLIE, Harold Gilmour	2nd Lieutenant	2nd Lieutenant	4th Battn. Royal Scots Fusiliers	—	—	Home Service
WYLIE, John	Private	Company Sergeant-Major	Royal Army Service Corps	—	—	France and Belgium, 1917–1918
WYLIE, William Naismith	Private	Lieutenant	Queen's Own Cameron Highlanders	Invalided, September 1918	—	France and Belgium, 1917–1918
WYLLIE, Matthew	2nd Lieutenant	Captain	6th Battn. Highland Light Infantry	Wounded, September 1916	—	Gallipoli, 1915 Egypt, 1916
✠ WYPER, James Stewart	2nd Lieutenant	Lieutenant	8th (Service) Battn. King's Own Scottish Borderers	Died of wounds, 8th September, 1916, in Rouen	—	France, 1915–1916
WYPER, John S.	Captain	Captain	5th Battn. Highland Light Infantry	—	—	France, 1917–1918

NAME.	RANK. At beginning of War or on joining.	RANK. At end of War.	UNIT.	CASUALTIES.	HONOURS OR DECORATIONS.	FIELD OF SERVICE.
YOUNG, Alfred A.	Captain	Captain	Royal Army Medical Corps	—	—	Home Service
YOUNG, D. Roy, M.B.	Lieutenant	Captain	Royal Army Medical Corps	Wounded	—	—
YOUNG, Edwin Lang	Able Seaman	Sub-Lieutenant	Royal Naval Volunteer Reserve	Invalided, November 1915, November 1916 and February 1917 Wounded, November 1918	—	Gallipoli, 1915 Imbros, 1916 France, 1916-1918
✠ YOUNG, Eric Templeton	Lieutenant	Captain	8th Battn. The Cameronians (Scottish Rifles)	Killed in action, 28th June, 1915	—	Gallipoli, 1915
YOUNG, George Ernest Robson	Cadet	2nd Lieutenant	28th (County of London) Battn. The London Regiment (Artists Rifles) 9th Battn. The Black Watch (Royal Highlanders)	Wounded, August 1917	—	France, 1917
YOUNG, J. Harold	Lieutenant-Commander	Commander	Royal Navy	—	—	At Sea, 1914-1918
YOUNG, James Maclaren	Captain	Major	The King's Own Royal Regiment	—	Mentioned in Despatches Distinguished Service Order French Medal of Honour	France and Flanders, 1915
YOUNG, James Roy Stephens	Private	Lieutenant	9th Battn. The Royal Scots (Royal Regiment) Royal Air Force	—	Distinguished Flying Cross	Mediterranean, 1917-1918 Caucasus, 1918

NAME.	RANK. At beginning of War or on joining.	RANK. At end of War.	UNIT.	CASUALTIES.	HONOURS OR DECORATIONS.	FIELD OF SERVICE.
YOUNG, John	Lieutenant	Captain	Royal Army Medical Corps	—	—	Egypt and Palestine, 1915–1918
YOUNG, John Graham	Captain	Major	9th (G.H.) Battn. Highland Light Infantry	—	—	Home Service
YOUNG, John R.	Major	Major	17th Battn. Highland Light Infantry	Wounded, July 1916	Mentioned in Despatches	France, 1915–1916
YOUNG, John Wark	2nd Lieutenant	Lieutenant	7th Battn. The Northumberland Fusiliers	Wounded, November 1916	—	France and Belgium, 1916
YOUNG, Kenneth M.	Lieutenant	Major	Royal Artillery	Invalided, September 1915	—	Gallipoli, 1915 Egypt and Palestine, 1916–1918
YOUNG, Roy F.	Lieutenant	Captain	Royal Army Medical Corps	Wounded, October 1914	Mentioned in Despatches Military Cross	France, 1914–1918
YOUNG, Thomas Guthrie	2nd Lieutenant	Lieutenant	Royal Engineers	Wounded, July 1915	—	Gallipoli, 1915
YOUNG, W. A.	Lieutenant	Captain	14th London Regiment (London Scottish)	—	—	—
YOUNG, William P.	Private	Chaplain 3rd Class	9th Battn. The Royal Scots (Royal Regiment) Royal Army Chaplains Department	Wounded, June 1915 Prisoner of War, March 1918	Mentioned in Despatches twice Distinguished Conduct Medal Military Cross	France and Belgium, 1915 and 1917–1918

NAME.	RANK.		UNIT.	CASUALTIES.	HONOURS OR DECORATIONS.	FIELD OF SERVICE.
	At beginning of War or on joining.	At end of War.				
✠ YOUNGER, David George	Private	2nd Lieutenant	17th Battn. Highland Light Infantry	Killed in action, 1st July, 1916, on the Somme	—	France, 1916
✠ YOUNGER, John Woodburn	Ambulance Driver	Ambulance Driver	British Red Cross Society	—	—	France, 1917–1918
✠ YOUNGER, Robert Govan	Private	Lance-Corporal	Royal Army Service Corps	Wounded, November 1917, at Passchendale Prisoner, 21st March, 1918 Died, 3rd April, at Avesnes-sur-Helpi	—	France, 1917–1918

www.ingramcontent.com/pod-product-compliance
Lightning Source LLC
Chambersburg PA
CBHW060421100426
42812CB00030B/3268/J